THE
CRANNOGS
OF SCOTLAND

AN UNDERWATER ARCHAEOLOGY

THE
CRANNOGS
OF SCOTLAND

AN UNDERWATER ARCHAEOLOGY

NICHOLAS DIXON

First published 2004
Reprinted 2023

The History Press
97 St George's Place,
Cheltenham, Gloucestershire GL50 3QB
www.thehistorypress.co.uk

British Library Cataloguing in Publication Data.
A catalogue record for this book is available from the British Library.

ISBN 978 0 7524 3151 2

Typesetting and origination by Tempus Publishing.
Printed and bound by TJ Books Limited, Padstow, Cornwall

CONTENTS

ACKNOWLEDGEMENTS

My career in underwater archaeology really began at the University of St Andrews where Professor Colin Martin gave me my first opportunity to work on both exciting shipwrecks and the crannogs that have become my life's work. It is often with regret that I have concentrated my efforts in the dark and peaty waters of Scotland's freshwaters and have had few opportunities to dive in the clear waters around the coast, but the richness of the lochs is a constant draw. I have dived on many types of site and with many underwater archaeologists and divers who have always been an exciting and dynamic group. I have seen the great developments in equipment and techniques that now make it possible for young divers to become involved in the unique business of underwater archaeology and the time now seems ripe for a real boom in the subject.

Many people have been involved with the excavation of Oakbank Crannog over the years. Some were involved for a few days and others throughout the whole time of the project. By far the greatest majority have been volunteers and without them it would not have been possible to reach the point where we are now. To all of them I owe an immense debt of gratitude for contributing their time, effort and equipment. They are too many to name individually but they know who they are, and so do I, and the value of their involvement is incalculable.

I would particularly like to thank Alan and Kath Douthwaite who have been solid supporters since our first meeting in 1979. I would also like to thank Major John Cunningham, and the successive owners of Oakbank Cottage, the late John MacLean, Sheila and George Reid and the Keydens for their interest and access to the site. I must also show my appreciation to all of the people of Fearnan village who have put up with the noise of our pumps and compressors through long summer days without complaint.

My sincere thanks are due to the present and past trustees of the Scottish Trust for Underwater Archaeology who help to keep the organisation true to its aims and objectives and give invaluable advice and support. The members of the STUA, and more recently the Friends of the Crannog, have given immense support in many different ways, from processing pottery to building models, and I must particularly thank Patrick and Mary Cave-Browne and Dave and Ruth Jones for their contributions.

I must thank the grant-giving bodies and all of those who have allowed the excavations to go ahead by contributing that most important element, money, and I hope they feel that their input has been well-spent: The Ellis Campbell Foundation, The Carnegie Trust, The Esmee Fairbairn Trust, Glenfiddich Living Scotland Awards, Historic Scotland, The Mac Robertson Trust, The MacTaggart Third Fund, The Moray Foundation, Perth & Kinross Council, Perth & Kinross Heritage Trust, The Russell Trust, The Gannochy Trust, the Tay Charitable Trust and Simpson and Marwick, W.S.

The hands-on mechanics of excavation underwater is exciting for those involved but much of the information that tells the story is done in the laboratory and I thank all the researchers and scientists who have contributed to the understanding and interpretation of the site. I have unashamedly exploited them as researchers carrying out their own studies and hope they feel the material from Oakbank has been a fair exchange for their efforts.

The ongoing Lawers survey is made possible by organisation and funding by the National Trust for Scotland, Historic Scotland and the Heritage Lottery Fund. It could not be carried out without the help of volunteer shorewalkers and shallow water divers and snorkellers, guided by a number of enthusiastic professionals. Thanks also go to all of these helpers and also to the land owners who kindly gave permission for us to survey the shoreline and shallows on their property.

The recently initiated Perthshire Crannog Survey is carried out with support from Perth and Kinross Heritage Trust and the permission of a number of land owners and has a productive and exciting future.

Last but by no means least, I would like to thank my wife, Barrie Andrian, who has made a great contribution to my research in many different ways and whose support has been invaluable. The part she plays in the study of crannogs through her work for the Scottish Trust for Underwater Archaeology and the Scottish Crannog Centre makes an immense contribution to the presentation and understanding of this invaluable national resource to thousands of schoolchildren, students and members of the public each year.

One

INTRODUCTION

Scotland has an immensely rich underwater heritage. Although a small country, it has more than 30,000 large and small lochs, 10,000 river and stream systems (Lyle and Smith 1994) and 69% of the UK coastline. Throughout the last 10,000 years that the country has been occupied, from Mesolithic times until today, these would have been seen as valuable resources by the inhabitants. Scotland has, by necessity, been trading with the Continent, the countries of the Atlantic Province and Scandinavia since the earliest times. Vessels from the Bronze Age to the Medieval galleys of the Lords of the Isles lie in the waters around Scotland. Galleons from the Spanish Armada and Dutch East Indiamen are to be found around the shores. Also, in the nineteenth century Scotland was the major country in the world producing steamships; the First World War German battle fleet lies in Scapa Flow, as do many ships from the Second World War.

While there are many exciting sites submerged in Scotland this book will concentrate on the submerged and partly submerged settlement sites known as crannogs. The name may suggest a type of site that is probably quaint and rarely discovered but nothing could be further from the truth. Crannogs are found throughout the country and they vary in size and shape enormously *(1)*. In one loch alone, for example – Loch Tay in the Southern Highlands – there are the remains of 18 crannogs ranging in size from about 8m to 80m across, and with occupation dating from the Early Iron Age, 2,500 years ago, to the recent past, only 300 years ago. Loch Awe in the Western Highlands has 20 crannogs with the same date range as Loch Tay, and there are 10 crannogs in Loch Lomond. Forty-eight sites in three lochs is impressive but with more than 30,000 lochs in Scotland the final count will be very much higher.

There may be a tendency to assume that such idiosyncratic-sounding sites represent a unique watery culture group. In some cases where communities live a life reliant on their watery surroundings this may be so. The Marsh Arabs of southern

1 Distribution of possible crannogs in Scotland, and lochs surveyed by the STUA.

Iraq on the Euphrates delta are an example. However, the differences that water makes to their environment is considerable compared to the communities in the surrounding areas which are substantially desert. It is almost inevitable that the environmental differences result in different cultural groups.

In Scotland, there are significantly different types of artificial islands ranging from the timber crannogs of the wooded southern half of Scotland to the stony island duns of the barren Outer Hebrides. Again, different environments have resulted in cultural differences which are readily definable. However, the people who lived on crannogs in Loch Tay cannot be seen as culturally different to the people living in round houses on the nearby flood plain of the River Tay or the Tay Valley further to the east. Neither can the island dun-dwellers in the Outer Hebrides be seen as culturally different from the surrounding shore-dwellers. Both water-based and shore groups exploit the same environment and that would determine details of their cultures more than the type of house they lived in.

However, there are clearly differences between the crannog-dwellers and even nearby shore-dwellers; and it is an important part of the ongoing crannog research of the Scottish Trust for Underwater Archaeology (STUA) at Edinburgh University to help to define the often subtle comparisons and contrasts between crannogs and other types of site in similar environments of Scotland.

A notable element for consideration is the difference in preservation between water-based and shore-based archaeological remains. A circular ring of stones on shore with few associated artefacts, may seem to represent a relatively poor way of life, whereas the massive amounts of organic remains and artefacts from an underwater crannog of the same period, may seem to represent a relatively rich and well-fed way of life; however it is almost certain that their economic basis was similar. It is only the excellent preservation of material underwater that makes the crannog seem richer.

In fact, the results of submerged crannog excavations may change attitudes to the general archaeological perception of how rich or poor a cultural group is. For example, a shore site where a great deal of decorated pottery is discovered may seem to represent a rich group but there is little or no evidence to suggest that the members of that community ate well or to show how much of the surrounding environment they exploited. The evidence from crannogs in wooded areas is that they had little use for pottery as they could carve all sorts of domestic utensils out of the abundant wood around them. The lack of pottery, the most ubiquitous find on most archaeological sites, might imply poverty of lifestyle but the preserved environmental evidence shows that it was very rich.

UNDERWATER ARCHAEOLOGY

Underwater archaeology has made a massive contribution to our understanding of ships, trade and people in history and prehistory. Despite this, it is having a long and difficult birth. Twenty-five years ago, with the underwater excavation of Henry VIII's flagship, the *Mary Rose,* and other underwater projects, it looked like underwater archaeology would gain credibility and become an established part of mainstream archaeology. However, for a number of reasons it has been struggling for recognition and has in many places been hijacked by salvage companies and treasure hunters looking to sell off cultural material for their private gain. As little as 20 years ago diving was a relatively exotic pursuit but now many students who come into university archaeology courses are already divers and have no fear of the underwater world. It is important that they are given proper training in the subject.

A blinkered attitude to underwater archaeology is readily apparent in many traditional archaeological agencies. This may be attributed to a general fear of working in such an unfamiliar environment as underwater and the differences of operation it presents to the familiarity of dry land. There is much less understanding of the submerged archeological resource and consequently less effort made in its protection and preservation. An overall lack of awareness has resulted in a massive difference in the handling of archaeological remains found on land and underwater. Regardless of the difference in perceptions and understanding of submerged archaeological material it should receive as much attention and protection as material found on land. Now in the twenty-first century, as recognition dawns, a significant effort is needed to readjust the balance so that all archaeology is treated with equal care before material of national importance is lost in the greater exploitation of the waters of the seas and lochs of Scotland.

THE SUBMERGED HERITAGE

The submerged archaeological heritage is represented by all cultural material found underwater. Scotland's underwater resource is as diverse as it is widespread, making it one of the richest in the world. Submerged cultural material is found in the inland waters of rivers and lochs, including dammed waters for reservoirs and hydro-electric power schemes, lakes, canals and wells. It is also found in intertidal zones, and in coastal and offshore waters. Artefacts and sites may have been deliberately deposited, accidentally lost, inundated, abandoned, constructed in the water or eroded from the coast or riverbanks. Most discoveries are accidental and include observations by beach walkers, finds in fishermen's nets and reports by divers. Less often, they are the results of deliberate search and survey projects although the situation is slowly beginning to change.

RISKS TO SUBMERGED SITES

Inland areas

All submerged cultural material in Scotland is at risk from a wide range of commercial, mechanical and chemical threats but it is not within the scope of this book to cover them all. However, the preservation of sites in inland waters is challenged by fish farms, watersports, agricultural run-off, pollution and acidification and the leisure industry associated with new developments, such as waterfront timeshares and marinas, is being carried out with little or no understanding of the destruction that can take place.

Fish farms are a potential source of both mechanical and chemical damage. The infrastructure associated with them, including boats and fish cages, can cause significant erosion and direct damage through collision. Raised nutrient levels and chemical additions for the prevention of diseases in fish can cause environmental damage to cultural as well as natural resources. Archaeological impact studies should be implemented whenever and wherever developments are planned in lochs known to contain submerged archaeological material, or where the presence of such material is suspected.

The increase in water sports as a leisure activity is a growing threat to sites through collision with, and the effect of wave action created by, jet skis, water skiers and powerful motor boats. The general availability of water transport of all forms allows easy access to island sites where campers and picnickers can inadvertently or deliberately cause damage. A crannog of prehistoric date, in Barean Loch, Kirkcudbrightshire provides one example of such a problem. Timbers at the water's edge and in the shallows were deliberately kicked out, damaging them and exposing a section of delicate organic deposits to erosion. Local residents attributed this vandalism to young campers who almost certainly were unaware of the damage they were causing to the submerged cultural heritage (Dixon 1989b). This is a matter of education and it is heartening to see that an understanding of crannogs, and the important part they play in the past in Scotland, is now covered in many primary and secondary schools.

The effect of raised nutrient levels and acidification from agricultural and forestry run-off of fertilisers now appears to be having a significant impact on the fragile timber and organic deposits of many crannogs. Historic Scotland launched a project in 1989 to examine this effect in lochs in the south-west of the country. Twenty timber samples were taken from six crannogs and some were seen to be visibly suffering attack from a wide range of micro-organisms. In Milton Loch, Dumfries and Galloway, piles and other timbers from a crannog excavated in 1950 (Piggott 1953) were riddled with holes and damage caused by freshwater plants, snails and wood-borers *(2)*. The effects of pollution and acidification have not yet been quantified but problems such as the severe algal blooms discovered in Loch Leven and other lochs may be as damaging to cultural resources as they are to aquatic and human life.

2 Biological attack on a timber exposed in 1950 Milton Loch Crannog excavation. *N. Dixon*

PROTECTING SUBMERGED SITES

Submerged monuments record

Scotland's lack of a specific inventory of underwater archaeological remains serves to highlight the vulnerability of this aspect of the nation's heritage. Damage and potential dangers to submerged sites cannot be quantified until the range of sites can be identified and quantified. Survey of Scotland's inland waters is important to enhance the existing record of crannogs and other features. From an archaeological point of view, the settlement record cannot be complete when significant numbers of sites are basically ignored. The size of the resource must be established to allow appropriate protection measures to be set in motion where required.

Wrecks and other features can be detected with sophisticated remote-sensing equipment. Remotely operated vehicles (ROV) can be deployed in water too deep or dangerous for divers. The same equipment can be used in lochs where visibility is reduced by high peat-content, while aerial photography is effective in the shallows of relatively clear lochs. The techniques of low technology survey based on snorkelling and diving practice are simple, inexpensive, and well-established (Dixon 1982b; Dean *et al* 1992).

Underwater excavation, whether motivated by research or rescue, will enhance a monuments record with information on site identification and interpretation.

Material remains from underwater archaeological sites are normally very well-preserved due to the anaerobic conditions in which they are found. Excavations, therefore, can almost be guaranteed to produce valuable archaeological data in the form of structure, artefacts and environmental evidence. Underwater excavation, particularly in shallow water, need not be expensive, however the costs of conservation and laboratory analysis of rich organic deposits are high. While the physical constraints imposed by diving and working in an alien environment may seem daunting, working underwater has some distinct advantages over working on, for example, a drained waterlogged site (Dixon 1991).

RAISING AWARENESS

Education and raising awareness are major themes for the development of underwater archaeology and the protection of the underwater heritage. Only by raising public awareness of the need to protect their increasingly vulnerable drowned heritage will it eventually become socially unacceptable to damage, sell off, or otherwise dispose of archaeological material.

The Scottish Trust for Underwater Archaeology is an independent charitable organisation (charity no. SCO18418) formed to promote the research, recording and protection of Scotland's underwater sites. Towards realising these aims, the Trust carries out surveys and excavations and tries to increase awareness in the underwater heritage through education, publication and exhibition. These aims are supported by The Scottish Crannog Centre in Loch Tay, created by the STUA, as an educational resource and visitor centre. The STUA also liaises with statutory and other organisations, including environmental groups, in an attempt to ensure that underwater archaeology is considered in management and conservation strategies. Introductory and familiarisation courses in underwater archaeology are offered at all levels.

Archaeology practised underwater needs no more justification than archaeology practised on land. Submerged archaeological sites as a resource are an immensely rich and important aspect of the nation's heritage, yet legislation, particularly local legislation, is severely limited and has been shown to be inadequate for the protection of a large part of the resource. On a number of occasions, we at the STUA have been approached to comment on new developments that will impact on the sea or loch bottom. On every occasion the developers, often local councils, have demanded only a desktop survey and never have they been prepared to countenance actual examination of the sea or loch bed in the threatened area. Clearly, this level of consideration is totally inadequate to protect the submerged cultural heritage. The National Monuments Record of Scotland and regional sites and monuments records allow land-based rescue surveys and excavations to be carried out in areas where known or suspected archaeological material may be jeopardised by development. Recognising that an unquantified but well-preserved range of cultural material lies throughout Scottish waters, the charting of our underwater heritage also must be considered a priority and incorporated into current strategies outlining the way forward in Scottish archaeology.

Two

BACKGROUND TO CRANNOGS AND LAKE-DWELLINGS

A wide range of submerged sites has now been recognised in bogs and lakes throughout the world. Some can be examined and excavated with no more than wellington boots and planks across the site to enable access while others are so deep that they require the use of scuba-diving equipment. The benefit of all these sites is the excellent state of preservation of organic materials, which is not found on dry land sites. The most productive sites are those which have been totally submerged and are never exposed above the water, since even occasional exposure is enough to cause both biological decay and mechanical damage to some extent.

Lake-dwellings throughout Europe were studied, comprehensively, from as early as the nineteenth century (Keller 1866). They are generally known as 'Swiss' but, although they are distributed widely throughout Switzerland, they are also found in other countries. Of course, national boundaries as they now exist had no meaning in the prehistoric period and geographical factors, such as the existence of lakes and their proximity to trade routes, were more likely to determine the siting of settlements.

The best reference when looking at the range of lake-dwelling sites is still Robert Munro's *Lake-dwellings of Europe* which was published in 1892 and was based on six Rhind lectures he gave in 1888. With two years to prepare them Munro spent the time going around the Continent looking at all the different sites and the museums where the material from them was held. The best indications of the magnitude of his work are the list of sites that he visited, running into hundreds, and the bibliography at the end of the book which gives 469 references from countries throughout

Europe. Many of the sites observed in the nineteenth century have not been examined since then but from the early references it is clear that the range of site types is very broad. It includes pile-dwellings with hundreds of piles and timbers; stone mounds that may or may not include timbers; and substantial islands that may be wholly artificial or modified natural features. They are found in Italy, France, Greece, Germany, Poland and in many other countries as well as Switzerland.

While most research into lake-dwellings is carried out through archaeological survey, interesting information is also found in written texts. Herodotus' *Histories* describe lake-dwellers in the north of Greece in the fifth century BC, who are therefore contemporary with Oakbank Crannog, Loch Tay, which is discussed in detail below. Herodotus wrote about Megabazus the Persian taking the Paeonian tribes in the north of Greece and how he was not able to subdue the people living in lake-dwellings on Lake Prasias:

> The tribes in the neighbourhood of Mt Pangaeum and on the lake itself were not subjugated by Megabazus ... though he did attempt the conquest of the latter. The houses of these lake-dwellers are actually in the water, and stand on platforms supported on long piles and approached from the land by a single narrow bridge. (Histories *Book V, Section 17*)

He also described details about the way of life of the people:

> Each member of the tribe has his own hut on one of the platforms, with a trap-door opening on to the water underneath. To prevent their babies from tumbling in, they tie a string to their legs.

It would be interesting to know whether there is any evidence left of the lake-dwellings in that area now.

SCOTLAND

TYPES OF ARTIFICIAL ISLAND IN SCOTLAND

Artificial islands were constructed in Scotland in the first millennium BC, as early as 600 BC, and some sites were inhabited up until the seventeenth century AD. Evidence from Loch Olabhat in North Uist *(3)* suggests that loch-dwellings, totally artificial or modified natural features, may have been constructed as early as the Neolithic period (see page 23). Few lochs have been systematically surveyed to establish the presence or quantity of sites in them although some 400 known or suspected sites are listed in the records of the

3 Eilean Domhnuill, Loch Olabhat a possible Neolithic crannog. *N. Dixon*

Royal Commission on the Ancient and Historical Monuments of Scotland (RCAHMS).

 Submerged settlement sites were first examined in the nineteenth century and since then they have all been considered under the name 'crannog'. However, given the range in type and date of artificial islands and submerged structures the term, as a definition, applies only in the most general sense. Overall site remains range in size from less than 10m to more than 100m in diameter. Survey and excavation of these sites is required in order to formulate a meaningful classification system and to determine settlement patterns. Research undertaken by the STUA and the Department of Archaeology at Edinburgh University is contributing to both an inventory and classification of such sites and the development of new research programmes in underwater archaeology will result in greater progress.

Crannogs

Crannogs may be described as artificial islands originally built of timber, utilising driven piles to create a platform above the water supporting a house or settlement

4 Artist's impression of a crannog. A. Braby

(4). Others may have been constructed of stone but it is difficult to see how an effective timber-based habitation could be constructed on top of a bare mound of stones. The almost total use of stone for building artificial islands is best seen in the Hebrides where there are few trees for construction. The Early Iron Age site of Oakbank Crannog in Loch Tay (see below) is an example of a crannog which started life as a timber structure. The site was inhabited for as much as 200 years and contains the remains of numerous phases of habitation. Some significant time after the initial occupation of the site, the mound of organic debris, which had built up around the piles supporting the dwelling, was covered with stones resulting in a form of stony mound common throughout the country.

  Added to this group may be sites originally constructed by piling brushwood, peat and other materials in the water to create an artificial island held together by the addition of piles driven into and around the mass of material. This structural sequence was first proposed by Robert Munro (Munro 1882). His work at Buston Crannog in Ayrshire and recent excavation there (Crone 1991) suggests that it might fall into this category *(5)*. Several hundred years later than Oakbank Crannog and others in Loch Tay, Buston Crannog's occupation dates may be significant to this type of site. In other words, the people of the Dark Ages may have used a different technique to construct their crannogs than those of the earlier Iron Age. However, it is hard to imagine why builders as skilled as those who created the circular mortice and tenon-jointed site shown in Munro's plans would base the site on a pile of brushwood, turf, earth and stones. Particularly as it would then be extremely difficult to drive piles through this mass of material.

It is not possible to construct a realistic classification of crannogs due to the lack of data relating to their form and function mainly because structural details are often buried under a mantle of boulders, structural debris, a mound of organic material and/or a stand of trees. Past researchers suggested a clear distinction between stone and timber-based sites but recent work in Scotland, described below, indicates by the results of excavation that both timber and stone phases are found on the same site and that the boulder cover, which is the criterion for defining stone crannogs, is a result of rebuilding or modifying existing timber crannogs. In fact, the structural sequence postulated by Robert Munro in the nineteenth century, and still accepted by many archaeologists in recent years (for example, Cunliffe 1978, 227), is questionable and alternatives are proposed below based on recent work.

Island Duns and Brochs

Island duns, and brochs on islands, are widely distributed throughout the Highlands and Islands of Scotland. They consist of artificial and modified natural islands with a foundation of stones and the remains of a dun or broch on top, usually connected to the shore by a stone causeway. They may have fulfilled the same function as crannogs in lochs on the mainland but were constructed of stone in response to the relatively treeless landscape in which they are located. Examples of this type are found on the Isle of Lewis in Loch an Duin, Shader *(colour plate 1)*; Loch an Duna, Bragar and in Loch Bharabhat, Cnip. It is possible that many of these island brochs and duns overlie the remains of earlier habitation.

5 View of Buston Crannog excavation in 1879. *After Munro*

6 Bragar Broch, Loch an Duna, Bragar, Isle of Lewis, with submerged mound in background.
N. Dixon

Only one island site of this type has been excavated underwater and this was undertaken in conjunction with land excavations at Dun Bharabhat, Cnip (see page 72). A survey of artificial islands, including underwater inspection, was carried out on Lewis in 1985 and showed a wide range of structures (Dixon and Topping 1986). The exciting results from Loch Bharabhat, Cnip show that it would be useful to expand this programme and carry out a complete survey of Lewis and Harris and the other Hebridean islands.

Stone mounds

In areas where island duns and brochs are widely distributed, there are a number of submerged mounds that do not support dun or broch structures. In appearance they resemble the same type of site as the mainland crannogs. Both island duns and submerged mounds are sometimes found in the same small loch, such as at Loch an Duin and Loch an Duna on Lewis, where substantial island duns are associated with submerged stone mounds nearby *(6)*. The relationship between the two groups is of considerable importance to the development of settlement types and patterns in the region, with the island duns dating to the Iron Age and later and the submerged mounds presumably dating to earlier periods as they are deeper. There is a clear impression that the substantial island duns were preceded by the submerged mounds.

Elsewhere, such mounds are the only site in a loch, for example, in Loch Airigh na Lic, near Stornoway. As there are no remains of stone buildings on the mounds it may be that they supported turf or timber buildings, or none at all. Alternatively, stone associated with buildings may have been robbed for the larger island-dun/broch sites where the two types exist together. Superficially the mounds are similar to the mainland crannogs and may even have had timber foundations in times when there were more trees available in these now barren areas but it will require excavation to fully clarify the situation.

Other submerged and partly submerged sites

There are also island mounds superficially resembling brochs and duns but of earlier or later date. The Neolithic site of Eilean Domhnuill, Loch Olabhat in North Uist is a good example of the type (Armit 1990) and if it was an artificial island it is the earliest in Scotland by far. The STUA carried out a small test excavation underwater and encountered a well-preserved hurdle, timber piles, animal bones, straw rope, and other organic remains below the levels reached in the land excavations. The true form of the island is not clear as a segment of walling is submerged nearby in the shallow waters some distance from the edge (Dixon 1989c) but there is a strong likelihood that the site was an island in the Neolithic period.

Freshwater transport, including logboats, steamships, and fishing boats, is typical of the other types of archaeological material found throughout Scottish inland waters. Other features include river crossings and canals, landing stages, fish traps and more modern structures which are now underwater through, for example, the damming of lochs for use as reservoirs and hydro-electric power schemes.

Maritime mounds

A number of apparently artificial islands resembling freshwater crannogs are located in the Clyde Estuary, the Beauly Firth and on the West Coast of Scotland. Four sites in the Beauly Firth date from the Iron Age although it is not clear whether they were crannogs or some other structure such as beacons. These sites are accessible from the shore at low tide, raising questions as to their effectiveness as defensive settlements although attempting to access them through thick mud is not easy and the mud itself offers a significant level of protection. It is interesting to consider the problems associated with constructing such settlements if they were subject to the same tidal flooding that occurs today. Research for a PhD, including survey and excavation of estuarine crannogs, was carried out by Alex Hale at Edinburgh University (Hale 1994). Further survey may locate similar sites elsewhere and more work is required to clarify their function and to place them in the context of other Scottish maritime communities.

Other sites exist in Scotland which at first sight may not appear to be crannogs but unless their foundations are examined there is no certainty that they were not constructed upon the remains of earlier artificial islands. These sites include some duns, brochs and Medieval stone castles all of which are found in Scottish lochs and are exemplified by Dun Breinish, Loch an Duin, North Uist (Blundell 1913), Clickhimmin Broch, Shetland (Hamilton 1968) and Loch Doon Castle, Ayrshire (Fairbairn 1937). These substantial stone sites may have required solid bedrock for a firm foundation but evidence from elsewhere suggests that this is not necessarily so. An island in the Loch of Kinellan, Inverness-shire, covering an area of about half-an-acre supported substantial stone buildings which were inhabited up to the late Medieval period, yet excavation showed that the main part of the island's foundation consisted of the remains of earlier timber structures and that it was completely artificial (see page 48) *(colour plate 2)*.

For the purposes of this work a crannog is considered to be any artificial or mainly artificial island which does not readily encroach upon the criteria defining other types of site such as those mentioned above. It is accepted that crannog remains may underlie these and other classes of monument and that this may be demonstrated by survey or excavation in the future. Such a tenuous definition is hardly satisfactory but until more work is carried out in this field it is not possible to be more exact.

Crannogs are usually placed under the heading of lake-dwellings and are seen as being in some way related to other sites throughout Europe with a lacustrine connection, no matter how tenuous. A brief outline of the sort of sites which are generally accepted as lake-dwellings in Britain and on the Continent shows their diversity and their contrast with crannogs in almost every case.

IRELAND

The only other country where many crannogs have definitely been identified is Ireland, with 400 sites known by 1957 (Raftery 1951, 37). There is little doubt that many of the Scottish and Irish sites are similar, according to the many observations and a number of excavations which have been carried out in the twentieth century. Systematic work was carried out by H.O. Hencken in the 1930s and '40s with massive excavations at Lagore and Balinderry crannogs (Hencken 1937, 1942, 1950). Overall, the evidence from Ireland is diverse, with a range of theories about form and dating. There are crannogs, certainly from the early Christian period and later and many lakeside settlements, possibly including crannogs, from the Mesolithic onwards (O'Sullivan 1998). However, other views place the origins of Irish crannogs around the fifth century AD with occupation lasting until the end of the Medieval period (Edwards 1990, Lynn 1983). The discussion is mainly one of the difference between lakeside sites and those actually built in the water. Certainly many of the Irish crannogs fall into the early Historic and Medieval periods and in this group are some very rich sites including the royal centre of Lagore which was examined archaeologically in 1839 (Wilde 1840) and was comprehensively excavated by Hencken.

It is not possible from the quality of the evidence so far available to establish the range of types of lake-dwelling found in Ireland but it seems to range from free-standing pile-dwellings to lakeside dwellings built on the edges of the loughs, which were later inundated. The latter are well displayed at Lough Eskragh, Co. Tyrone (Williams 1978) where both crannogs and lakeside sites are in evidence but the number and position of habitation areas in the waters around the edge of the lough suggest that it may have been smaller during earlier periods at which time these sites would have been on shore, at the water's edge.

In Ireland, Lagore Crannog may in some structural aspects relate to the Scottish sites but as a rich royal dwelling it is not even culturally representative of most other Irish crannogs. Many of the Irish sites of a less exotic nature than Lagore, such as those listed by Wood-Martin (1886, 163ff), may be more characteristic of the Scottish ones. According to the description a crannog in Lough Ravel, Co. Antrim accords well with many of the Scottish references. It was about 38 yards in diameter, surrounded by oak piles with morticed cross-timbers. The interior was built-up of wood and earth and flat fire-marked stones suggest the presence of a hearth. Finds from the site did not indicate particularly poor inhabitants and included wooden and copper dishes, bronze spear-heads and daggers and iron implements. Decorated glass beads and a silver brooch suggest that the inhabitants were relatively well-off compared to those of many Scottish sites. The author stated that finds from the site were '…sold from time to time to various collectors' (Wood-Martin 1886, 163) a practice apparently common in Ireland at the time, according to the text.

The time range, the variety of forms and the sheer quantity of the Irish sites makes it impossible to do more here than indicate the potential of the material. Systematic work is going on there under the auspices of the Discovery Programme and others and the potential of these sites for work to the highest standards is clear. The excellent book on Irish crannogs, *The Archaeology of Lake Settlement in*

Ireland by Aidan O'Sullivan, is essential reading for anyone interested in looking further into the Irish sites (O'Sullivan 1998).

ENGLAND

A number of so-called pile-dwellings have been recorded from England but none of them, on examination of the literature, indicates the existence of sites like crannogs. A number of small meres, or bogs, in Suffolk and Norfolk when drained in the past have been shown to have bones of animals and timber piles embedded in the bottom (Munro 1882, 290) but no reports of distinct timber-framed mounds are recorded. A site at Barmston, Holderness, East Yorkshire was regarded as a pile structure and possible lake-dwelling (Munro 1882, 301) but recent work has shown that it was not built in the same way as a crannog.

The important and extensive Iron Age sites of Glastonbury and Meare in the Somerset Levels have been shown through recent evaluation to have been built on areas of peat, and in the case of Meare, some distance from open water. These were extensive villages without the form of artificial islands and possibly with a wider diversity of functions than the great majority of crannogs. Their occupation at a time when Scottish sites were also in use emphasises a general exploitation of abundant wetlands at that time and the fact that such sites did not apparently persist in England long after the first two centuries of the first millennium AD points as much to substantial changes in the landscape through agricultural exploitation as to cultural developments.

Discoveries of a timber platform at Flag Fen in Cambridgeshire were first thought to be those of a crannog but further excavations showed that it was probably a more extensive structure and not formed as an artificial island as such (Pryor 1991). Still, it demonstrates the almost self-evident use of piles and beams for building dry platforms in wet areas.

WALES

The only crannog recognised outside of Scotland or Ireland was first reported in the nineteenth century in Llangorse Lake, Brecon, Wales *(7)*. The site was apparently an island in the lake with a stockade, timber floor and deposits of charcoal and food-refuse (Munro 1890, 464). The site was examined in recent years and a timber platform and oak palisade were uncovered dating to the ninth century AD. Unfortunately, living floors and house plans could not be ascertained because of erosion within the palisaded area but abundant evidence of occupation was seen by discoveries of charcoal, burnt bone, rings of shale and glass, whetstones, beads and half of a bone comb. Slag and crucibles suggest that metalworking was taking place on the site and agriculture is indicated by carbonised grain and part of a

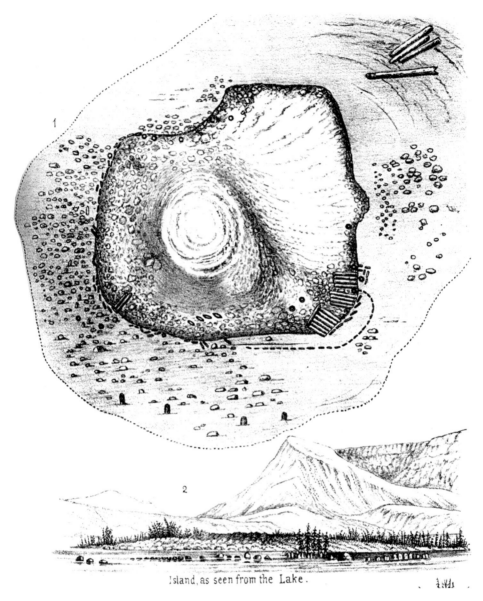

Island, as seen from the Lake.

7 Early drawing of the crannog in Llangorse Lake. *After Keller*

quern. A substantial number of artefacts, from a wide range of dates, came from the silts around the site and included the remains of a fine textile and the hinge from a reliquary indicating that the site had been a high-status royal residence with similarities to the later Irish crannogs (Redknap and Lane 1994). Work continues at Llangorse Lake with more excavation planned.

CONTINENTAL LAKE-DWELLINGS

In continental Europe a large number of submerged sites have been discovered in recent years and work has taken place on many of the sites recognised in the nineteenth century (Munro 1890).

The most commonly recorded lake-dwellings and those which are best known are the sites in Switzerland. As early as the seventeenth century fishermen and antiquarians knew of the existence of masses of timbers in many locations and often collected antiquities from the lake-bed with the use of forked poles. However, it was in 1854 when the lake levels fell unusually low that the full extent of the sites and the well-preserved archaeological material from them was realised. They were originally reconstructed by Ferdinand Keller as free-standing pile-dwellings built over the water and isolated from the shore except for a wooden gangway *(8)* (Keller 1866, 3-8). However, he had never excavated a lake-dwelling and most of his conclusions came from the work of anthropologists and ethnographers working in places like New Guinea at the time, who observed people still living on pile-dwellings.

A great deal of research has been carried out regarding the Swiss sites and it is now clear that they were, in fact, built and rebuilt during a number of periods on the sides of the lakes and were never surrounded by open water except during floods, at which time they were abandoned (Ruoff 1980, 148). There is therefore little structural comparability with the Scottish and Irish sites. Dr Ruoff (the State archaeologist for the canton of Zurich) who has been intimately involved in the Swiss work since the early 1960s, and who visited Scotland to look at crannogs in 1979, admits to never having seen a site like a Scottish crannog in Swiss waters.

The great majority of lake-dwellings so far discovered in Europe compare with the Swiss sites and contrast with the crannogs but a discovery at Fiave, Trentino, Italy, shows that pile structures did exist in open water in the Bronze Age (Ruoff 1980, 149). A timber platform supported by piles, as much as 9m long, extended from a small island into the lake, but even in this case the site is an appendage to an existing natural feature and built from a different structural form than the crannogs.

Crannogs were once seen as western outliers of the Central European lake-dwelling group; now they can be viewed as a type of site restricted in distribution to Scotland and Ireland and therefore important in clarifying the cultural development of the people in these countries. The construction of crannogs is no longer seen as a borrowing from outside but as a concept initiated and developed by the indigenous population.

Ferdinand Keller, in the nineteenth century, pointed out that the Swiss sites were not contemporary with those in Britain and this appeared to be the case until recently. However, modern dates from Zug, Switzerland and Oakbank,

IDEAL SKETCH of a SWISS LAKE-DWELLING.

8 Reconstruction of Swiss Lake village from 1866. *After Keller*

Scotland show that these two sites are contemporary (Ruoff 1980, 148), although the majority of Swiss sites are Neolithic and Early Bronze Age and therefore much earlier than dated British sites.

The number and range of sites in Ireland and elsewhere in Europe and the artefacts from them is too great to cover adequately here but it is sufficient to point out that there are significant differences between them all. Even a selection of sites is not necessarily representative and it is of little value to this work to detail elements of sites which are related to Scottish crannogs merely by being beside water.

Three

SCOTTISH CRANNOGS: BACKGROUND

Much of the evidence from Scottish crannogs points to their use as secure settlements with an economy based on agriculture and inhabitants who practised a range of craft industries. This general description could be applied to many of the small settlement sites, such as brochs, duns, palisaded settlements and hut-circles found throughout Scotland; so the evidence from one type may well be of relevance to the understanding of others. However, the size of crannogs varies much more than most of the other sites and it may be that in cases where large and small crannogs are found in close proximity, as in the case of Loch Tay (see below), some evidence of specialised functions or social structure may be implied. For example, there are a number of sites called Eilean nan Con which means Dog Island. It is possible that they were kennels for housing packs of hunting dogs.

The fact that farming was carried out is shown by numerous finds of querns; pollens of cereal and weeds of cultivation; and well-preserved ards —a sort of primitive plough – for tilling the ground, from Milton Loch (Piggott 1953, 143) and Oakbank Crannog in Loch Tay. Animal bones from many sites indicate the type of animals kept and their exploitation for food, textiles and implements of bone and horn. Craft industries ranged from spinning and weaving shown by finds of spindle whorls and loom weights, to carpentry and joinery in both the tools and the products in the form of wooden artefacts and structural timbers. Metalworking, probably small-scale bronze casting, since ore-smelting would be too complex and dangerous on a timber island, is displayed in the form of crucibles, slag and in the case of Buston Crannog in Ayrshire, globules of gold (Munro 1882). This may imply both mining and smelting on shore sites associated with the crannogs.

Results of research in the nineteenth century indicated the use of crannogs from the Roman Iron Age to the Medieval period but modern research shows that they were built as early as the Early Iron Age, or even earlier, in Scotland. Radiocarbon dates and finds testify to occupation from the seventh or eighth centuries BC to the seventeenth century AD and at almost every stage between these dates. Although many of the later sites may have been substantially stone-built, and certainly had stone buildings on them, many of the earlier artificial islands supported timber structures. Crannogs seem to have been the longest-lasting type of defended homestead in Britain. It is likely that the protection they were built to offer was primarily for the safety of the humans but they would also have helped to protect livestock from wolves, bears and wild cats which would have been common in Scotland at the time; evidence from Oakbank clearly shows that domesticated animals were taken out to the crannog. Crannogs would also allow grain to be stored in rodent-free conditions and many people have pointed to the possibility of midge-free conditions on sites away from the shore.

The original times when crannogs were built are not yet clear but so far the majority of radiocarbon dates are in the latter part of the first millennium BC; from 600 BC – AD 0. The dates used in this book are uncalibrated radiocarbon dates and, when the errors and inconsistencies of the method are taken into consideration, the date ranges can be plus or minus up to 200 years. Nevertheless, most of the crannogs that have been scientifically dated were built in the Iron Age and they were, at least in part, timber structures, which is not surprising as it was the existence of the timbers that allowed the dates to be calculated in the first place. If there is such a thing as an all-stone crannog it could be very difficult to date as radiocarbon dating needs organic material to work on.

In the past, finds from sites were used to date them and often these finds were from the top of the site or even the loch bed surrounding it. However, objects could have been lost by people just visiting old sites and they are not the best method of dating unless they are found clearly embedded in the structure. A number of crannogs in the past have been dated by finds to later than their true date of construction. That was clearly shown in the case of Milton Loch Crannog which is discussed below. Sites were used over a long period of time and people who lived on shore will often have gone back to the old crannog out in the water for protection in times of conflict and danger. It is possible that a timber crannog built in the Iron Age, was re-used in the Roman Period and the Dark Ages, was rebuilt of stone in the Medieval Period, possibly with a stone castle built on it, and was even used as a summer home in the seventeenth century AD. It is unlikely that timber crannogs were being built in the seventeenth century as their remains would still be substantial and, according to recent survey work, that is not seen to be the case. The only way to date the original construction of a crannog is to take a timber sample from the lowest part of the site that can be reached. One of the main benefits of loch-dwellings is that they were built in the water and the bases of most are still under water, preserving original structural timbers that can now be radiocarbon dated.

The reasons why people would go to the trouble of building artificial islands in water, sometimes more than 5m deep, may be more than for safety alone. The location of many crannogs suggests that they were deliberately sited off an area of cultivable land. It may have been necessary to clear woodland and shrubs before cultivation could begin and the cut timbers would supply the material for building the crannog. In order to utilise the cleared ground as soon as possible a house which did not encroach upon that space would be an advantage and the task of transporting timbers to the site would be easier if they could be floated out. As relevant a reason for this is the status related to constructing and inhabiting a complex structure like a crannog. The people who lived on these sites were making no effort to hide as they can usually be seen from miles around. It is much more likely that they are making a statement of strength and authority, standing up to be counted in the face of possible hostility. It is unlikely that any small-scale bandits and robbers would be prepared to attack groups who were demonstrably so powerful and organised.

Work in the late nineteenth and early twentieth centuries led to the conclusion that crannogs were concentrated in the south-west of Scotland, however this is related to the emphasis of archaeological work carried out at that time in the area. Modern surveys show that the concentration in the Highlands is no less than that in the Lowlands. Since lochs have not, in many cases, been affected by industrial development in the same way as on land, it is almost certain that a higher percentage of crannogs than land sites will be preserved. Although lochs were drained for agricultural purposes, particularly in the eighteenth and nineteenth centuries, there is likely to have been much less overall destruction than on good cultivable soils.

Another important aspect of the wide distribution of crannogs is that they are shown to overlie the boundaries of accepted artificial and natural divisions of Scotland. They are found in both the highland and lowland areas but they are also found in three of the four provinces described by Piggott in his *Scheme for the North British Iron Age* (1966) and can provide tests for the accuracy of such divisions in cultural terms since not only will exotic durable objects and structures be conserved, the criteria used by Piggott, but also a wide range of domestic paraphernalia made of wood and other organic materials.

It is one of the most important aspects of the remains of artificial islands that organic materials, from delicate textiles to massive timbers, are in an excellent state of preservation due to their waterlogged state. The importance of wood to prehistoric and later communities for fuel, implements and domestic and industrial tools has long been recognised. However, comparatively few sites can offer the conditions required for preservation. The number and distribution of crannogs means that a great range of well-preserved material is now available for study.

It is quite remarkable, then, that a brief appraisal of the modern archaeological literature will show that crannogs are hardly mentioned either as a wide-ranging group of settlement sites or as repositories of well-preserved organic material. This was not always the case. In the late nineteenth century when Robert Munro was at his peak concentrating on crannogs, they were an important and well-recognised type of site. By 1914 the subject of lake-dwellings was considered important enough to justify an entry of more than 17,000 words in the *Encyclopedia of Religion and Ethics*. In 1935 and 1940 in *The Prehistory of Scotland* and *Prehistoric Communities of the British Isles*, Gordon Childe, the first Professor of Prehistoric Archaeology at Edinburgh University, still saw crannogs as a significant element in the archaeological record though in the 1940 volume he laid the emphasis on the rich Irish sites and Glastonbury.

In 1949, Stuart Piggott, the second Professor of Archaeology at Edinburgh University, in *British Prehistory* referred to crannogs as circular houses on a platform of timber and brushwood '... in the Glastonbury manner, but a sufficiently obvious and common technique to have little or no cultural significance' (p 183). The references to crannogs were couched in terms of their similarity to sites in the Isle of Man, Ireland and England and by 1962 in *The Prehistoric Peoples of Scotland*, he made no reference at all to crannogs. Leslie Alcock, as a specialist in the Dark Ages, discussed them in *Arthur's Britain* but emphasised the wealth of the Irish royal sites in particular (Alcock 1971, 257). It is notable that all of the archaeologists writing in the twentieth century describe crannogs in the terms laid out by Robert Munro in *Ancient Scottish Lake-dwellings* (1882). In the last 40 years few writers have considered crannogs in other than a cursory manner although new young researchers are beginning to take an interest in them once more.

The reason why interest in crannogs fell off after the 1940s and why they still receive such little consideration is easy to understand. In the 1930s when Childe was writing, the work of Munro was still considered with some reverence. By the 1960s, modern methods and techniques had thrown suspicion upon the primitive methods of antiquarians and early archaeologists. No systematic studies on the subject had replaced Munro's work so rather than court contention by still quoting research based on questionable methods, the subject was left open. And the reason why no modern systematic research has been carried out on crannogs until recently is because they are still islands surrounded by water or are totally submerged.

There are various reasons why the time is right now for further work on the artificial islands of Scotland. Recent survey work and reappraisal of the sites has shown that there may be many more than 500 crannogs throughout the country. To consider the settlement pattern and cultural development of prehistoric Scotland without including such a large number of settlement sites is likely to produce a very incomplete picture. The watery location of the crannogs restrained researchers throughout the twentieth century, but modern developments in technology now make it possible to carry out efficient and accurate survey and excavation underwater with the prospect of impressive results. Survey and excavation carried out in Loch Tay has established the feasibility, cost-effectiveness and archaeological value of underwater work on crannogs.

In the nineteenth century considerable research was carried out on crannogs. This is outlined in some detail, particularly the contribution of Robert Munro and the conclusions he reached regarding the origins, structure and inhabitants of Scottish crannogs. His valuable work represented the only systematic research on the subject for decades. The contribution of Rev. F. Odo Blundell in the first decade of the twentieth century and his underwater exploits is also notable. Five excavations of crannogs took place in the twentieth century and occasional surveys were carried out with varying results. Most of the past work has had no lasting impact in the archaeological record but deficiencies of that work can now be overcome using modern methods and techniques of excavation in conjunction with developments in working underwater.

Four

EARLY NOTICES OF CRANNOGS IN SCOTLAND

Crannogs were noted in the early records from at least the eighteenth century. Many of the references are included in the *Old* and *New Statistical Accounts of Scotland* from the eighteenth and early nineteenth centuries respectively. While these references were by no means historical or archaeological accounts they do add some interesting information regarding how these sites were considered by the people of the time.

THE *OLD STATISTICAL ACCOUNT*

The *Old Statistical Account of Scotland* compiled in the late eighteenth century and the *New Statistical Account* of the early nineteenth century included a number of records. Lochrutton, Loch Kinder and Carlingwark in Kirkcudbright are mentioned in the earlier Account as is one of the Highland lochs, Loch Spinie in Morayshire. Lochrutton and Loch Kinder were reported as containing islands which stand above the surface and are apparently artificial. Presumably the reporter had made specific efforts to examine the sites as the island in Lochrutton (OSA vol. ii, 37) is in the middle of the loch some 200m or more from shore. Also, he must have attempted to observe their submerged features since he records them as being constructed of large stones on foundations of oak timber frames, stating that the woodwork in Loch Kinder '... is visible when the weather is clear and calm'. (OSA vol. ii, 139) An underwater examination of the island in Lochrutton in 1979 established that oak piles and horizontal timbers are still evident on the loch bed at the base of the mound though none were observed on the surface. Radiocarbon dates from samples taken in 1991 placed the site in the Medieval Period. Most of the sites in Carlingwark Loch (OSA vol. viii, 304) and the one in Loch Spinie (OSA vol. x, 625) came to light when the lochs were lowered by draining.

Carlingwark is of particular interest since two islands stood above the surface prior to lowering of the water and a number of crannogs were exposed afterwards. It is not clear from the report how many submerged sites were eventually discovered but there are references to at least five (Munro 1882, 29).

A causeway of stone led to one of the existing islands and was strengthened by oak piles which may suggest the use of timbers in the island itself. A number of canoes were found in the loch and other finds included stags' heads, a gold-plated dagger and many horseshoes. Later finds are recorded, in particular a bronze cauldron containing implements of iron and bronze of Roman date, which is believed to be a votive hoard.

Loch Spinie, Morayshire, is the only crannog recorded in the *Old Statistical Account* from the Highland area. It was described as a small artificial island '60 paces by 16' and apparently constructed of quarried stones 'bound together by crooked branches of oak' (Munro 1882, 30).

THE *NEW STATISTICAL ACCOUNT*

The *New Statistical Account* makes reference to two other sites in the south-west of the country. 'Firm stakes of oak and elm' were embedded in the bottom of the Loch of Boghall, Ayrshire and may represent the remains of a crannog though they are recorded as being used for fixing fishing nets (Munro 1882, 30). In the parish of Culter, Lanarkshire in a bog was an oval mound known as Greene Knowe about 30 x 40 yards with the remains of a stone causeway leading to the shore. It was composed of stones through which a great number of 1m-long oak piles had been inserted.

Highland lochs are also represented in the *New Statistical Account*. Loch Rannoch, Perthshire is attributed two small islands of which one is wholly artificial and founded on large beams of wood fixed to each other (NSA vol. x, 539). There is reputedly a narrow causeway underwater leading to the south shore but this was not evident during a visit in 1980, although in 1985 when the loch level was very low it was possible to wade to the site in knee-deep water. Survey carried out by the STUA in 2004 has shown this to be a very exciting site and the results of samples taken for radiocarbon dating are eagerly awaited. An island in the Loch of Kinellan, Ross-shire, was recorded as being based on logs of oak and having been at one time a house of strength (see page 48) and remains of a stone building were reported on an artificial island in the Loch of Achilty, Ross-shire.

The early references (cited above from the 1791-99 and 1845 *Statistical Accounts*) although in most cases of a cursory nature, indicate a number of elements common to many crannogs examined then and subsequently. Many of these common elements used to identify the artificiality of the islands in the past are the same features recognised by crannog surveyors today.

Piles were often recorded, usually identified as oak, and sometimes joined to transverse timbers with mortice and tenon joints. The timbers were frequently described as being made of 'black oak', as in the case of the frames from Carlingwark; 'bog oak' or, as in Greene Knowe, 'oak of the hardest kind'. The heart of oak which is submerged turns black and can survive in open water where other, softer woods erode away. Preserved oak timbers projecting from submerged crannog mounds may be the only external evidence that they have an internal timber framework.

Timbers which were still attached to each other, such as those from the loch in the parish of Croy, Nairnshire (the Loch of the Clans, see page 41) or those displaying the remains of mortice joints, were clearly man-made but even where no joints remain there may be the evidence of tool-marks on pointed stakes, such as those found at Greene Knowe.

In many cases, although it is seldom specifically stated, the layer of stones and the underlying timbers were seen as forming a single phase of construction. This is a relatively simplistic view of what are very complicated sites and it is likely that in many cases timber and stone phases relate to different phases of occupation at different times. This is not to say that in some cases stones and timbers were not used in conjunction but that was not necessarily the case, and a false impression has been produced which suggests that most crannogs were constructed of alternating layers of stones, brushwood, earth and timbers.

The early reference to Carlingwark Loch suggested that a number of crannogs may have been inhabited in relatively close proximity in the form of a more or less united community or hamlet. The same situation was seen when the Loch of Dowalton was drained in 1863 and five crannogs were exposed as well as six smaller stone-covered mounds. Modern surveys of Loch Awe, in 1972, and Loch Tay, in 1979, proved the existence of 20 and 18 definite crannogs respectively. However, unless sites are reliably dated it is not possible to say that they are associated with one another even though they are located close together.

The early recorders of the *Old* and *New Statistical Accounts* did not show surprise at the existence of artificial islands. Occasionally they referred to local traditions, such as that relating to Carlingwark Loch which talked of '...a town in the loch which sank, or was drowned' (OSA viii, 304), or the statement regarding Loch Rannoch that 'This island was sometimes used as a place of safety in cases of emergency; at other times, as a place of confinement for such as rebelled against or offended the chief' (NSA x, 539).

9 Loch Clunie island, Perthshire, with castle surrounded by dense undergrowth. *N. Dixon*

The impression may be given by later writers that artificial islands were neither known of nor considered until brought to public knowledge by the antiquarians of the second half of the nineteenth century, however, it should be remembered that many crannogs were inhabited into the post-Medieval period. An artificial island in Loch Ternate, Arisaig, was traditionally a place of refuge for criminals who, if they could get permission from the local chief and stay on the island for 48 hours, would be free from punishment (Blundell 1913, 290). There are many other references to local traditions which relate to islands, artificial and natural, and the reporters who recorded the information for the early *Statistical Accounts* were relatively close in time to the crannogs when they were still in use.

It may be argued that crannogs have been utilised and known of in Scotland since the prehistoric period and that any hiatus in that continuity is more apparent than real. When lake-dwelling studies reached a peak in the last half of the nineteenth century, the early reports were overshadowed by the work done then and it appeared that as a type of site they were being considered for the first time. Certainly they were being examined in detail for the first time but, as integral elements of the Scottish landscape as settlements, ruins, or the subject of folklore and tradition, they had been commonly accepted possibly from as early as the Bronze Age through the post-Medieval period.

Supporting this position are the many charters and tacks which refer to islands throughout the last millennium and their inclusion in official acts and ordinances. Records relating to the subjugation of the Western Isles of Scotland state:

> That the haill houssis of defence strongholdis and cranokis in the Yllis perteining to thame and their foirsaidis sal be delyverit to his Maiestie ... (Regist. Secreti Concilii: Acta penes Machianum et Insularum Ordinem *1608–23, pp 4–5, Munro 1882, 19*)

Currently in Scotland, research is being carried out by Matthew Shelley, a PhD student in Archaeology at Edinburgh University, into the Medieval and later islands and a wealth of exciting information is being revealed from close examination of early records and particularly from old maps, followed up by site surveys in the field. The work is showing clearly that artificial islands were an integral part of the settlement record well into the eighteenth century and there are even a number of sites that were inhabited into the twentieth century, such as the castle on a small island in Loch Clunie, Perthshire *(9)*.

Five

ARCHAEOLOGICAL INTEREST IN SCOTLAND

Archaeological interest in Scottish crannogs began at the beginning of the nineteenth century, stimulated by a paper published on Irish crannogs in the *Proceedings of the Royal Irish Academy* by Sir W.R. Wilde in 1840 (Wilde 1840) and by revelations in the Swiss lakes where many structural piles came to light due to a drought in 1853-54. Work really only began to develop with the formation of the Society of Antiquaries of Scotland and the publication of the Proceedings of their meetings from 1854. Indeed the first volume included a report of the discovery of some Roman bronze vessels from the Loch of Leys, Kincardineshire where a crannog is also recorded. It was occupied by the Wauchopes, then the Burnetts, during the Medieval period, probably inhabiting stone buildings at that time, but the superstructure of the island is based on oak and birch timbers (Munro 1882, 26-27).

The *Proceedings of the Society of Antiquaries of Scotland* (PSAS) gave the opportunity to report finds that had been made in earlier years. For example, in 1858, John Mackinlay presented to the Society descriptions of two crannogs which he had examined in Bute in 1812 and 1814 respectively. One was in Dhu Loch and was constructed of piles and transverse beams with an infill of moss and turf and a cover of '… shingle, or quarry rubbish, to form a floor' (Mackinlay 1860, 44); the other was in Loch Quein and was, according to Mackinlay, a natural structure with a stone wall around the periphery but with a double row of piles flanking a line of stones which formed a causeway to the shore (Mackinlay 1860, 45).

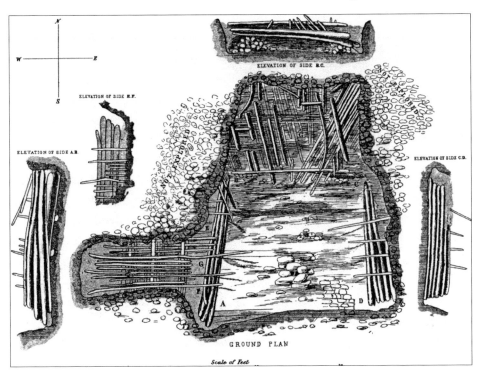

10 Plan from original excavation of crannog in Loch of the Clans. *After Munro*

THE LOCH OF THE CLANS:
THE FIRST SCOTTISH CRANNOG EXCAVATION

In 1863 the remains of two crannogs were observed in a drained area of the Loch of the Clans in Nairnshire by Dr J. Grigor (Grigor 1863). He recorded seeing oak timbers and branches projecting from a mound, which he referred to as a cairn, within the margin of the old loch. He thought upward sloping timbers were the rafters of an upright roof *(10)* and noted a layer 'of charcoal and burnt vegetable matter, along with small bits of bone', clearly habitation debris, in a part of the site which had been disturbed by the farmer. He did not doubt that it was the remains of 'an insular dwelling, a wooden castle' and he thought it was for '... safety from the wild beasts of the surrounding forests, or for the convenience of the hunter'. 50m from this site he recorded another area of stones surrounded by piles with evidence of hearth stones in the centre overlying charcoal and fragments of bone representing the remains of a second crannog.

Grigor returned to the first site later in the year to carry out excavation and established to his own satisfaction that he had indeed uncovered the rafters of a roof. Further work revealed a roughly square room with four upright walls standing about 1m high. The wood was oak from trees about 30 years old. The floor of the house was the bottom of the old loch and outside the 'walls', underneath the sloping-up rafters he found burnt wood, charcoal and peat-dross mixed with small seeds like buckwheat. Grigor believed the stones which overlay the timbers were there to hold down the ends of the rafters and to strengthen the structure. He acknowledged that the foundation must have been below water and states that:

> ... the distribution of the beams and cross beams, and the remnants of beam filling below, evidently appear to have been done with the intention of keeping out the water. (*Grigor 1864, 333*)

It seems highly unlikely that the excavated remains of the first crannog in the Loch of the Clans represented, as Grigor stated, the roof structure and walls of a house particularly with a floor on the loch bed. It is more likely to have been the substructure of an artificial island from which the superstructure had been eroded. Grigor, at that date, had seen no comparable sites and had no standards to apply to his work so it is not surprising if he misconstrued the form of the structure. This excavation was notable as the first of a crannog in Scotland.

JOHN STUART AND THE LOCH OF DOWALTON

Grigor's work was only just the first crannog excavation as four months later similar research was being carried out in Wigtownshire in the south-west of the country by Lord Lovaine who reported his findings to the British Association for the Advancement of Science at its 1863 meeting in Newcastle. He examined a number of sites which had come to light when the Loch of Dowalton was drained. Five were substantial crannogs, according to his description, and six were small stone mounds which he identified as single dwellings. Two canoes were also exposed: one 7.3m and the other 5.6m long.

When Lord Lovaine examined the sites in the Loch of Dowalton the loch bed was still wet and muddy with standing water in places but by 1864 the bed was dry and John Stuart, the secretary of the Society of Antiquaries of Scotland, carried out further observations and excavation. He first examined a site called Millar's Cairn which demonstrated many of the features recognised in the early Scottish accounts and compared favourably with many of the Irish examples. The mound was surrounded by numerous rows of piles cut from young oak trees and at one side were:

> morticed frames of beams of oak, like hurdles, and below these, round trees laid horizontally. In some cases the vertical piles were morticed into horizontal

bars … The hurdle frames were neatly morticed together, and were secured by pegs in the mortice holes. (*Stuart 1866, 116*)

Three superimposed clay deposits 'browned and calcined, as from the action of fire', were the remains of successive hearths and animal bones and wood ash were found in association. The three hearths show that the site had been occupied for a considerable period of time.

Well-preserved organic material was noted by Stuart in the form of 'perfectly distinct' hazel leaves and nuts and hazel branches on which the bark still remained. Ferns and heather 'looked as if recently laid down'.

Animal bones from the sites in Dowalton Loch showed evidence of cattle, pigs and sheep or goats and the bone of a large bird was also seen. A number of finds from the sites and from the loch bed included bronze dishes (one with the name CIPIPOLIE on the handle) and glass beads pointing to a habitation phase during the Roman period.

Stuart was of the opinion that analogies existed between the Scottish and Irish crannogs and those at Dowalton. On shore near many of the Irish sites were raths (small stone forts) and Stuart believed that shore sites would exist near Scottish crannogs as well. He gave as an example a crannog in Loch Lomond with a castle nearby, which is probably Strathcashel Point on the east shore of the loch, but the same association is not generally seen elsewhere.

THE FIRST COMPILATION OF CRANNOGS IN SCOTLAND

John Stuart made a list of what he believed to be all of the crannogs known in Scotland. He incorporated notes from an unpublished paper read by Joseph Robertson to the Society in 1857, the results of the work done in the Loch of Dowalton and all the other observations of crannogs which he could trace and produced them as a paper for the Society's proceedings in 1866. His work is recognised as the first systematic compilation of Scottish crannogs and Stuart also made comparisons with lake-dwellings from Ireland and the Continent (Stuart 1866).

Within 20 years of Stuart's paper it was established that sites with substructures like those in Dowalton existed elsewhere (Munro 1882) and debate developed regarding the structural techniques employed in the construction of artificial islands and the range of types of sites that were known.

The researchers at this time would not be classed as archaeologists now and were antiquarians with a lively interest in many aspects of history. Notwithstanding the superficiality of the early work, by the late 1870s it was generally accepted that a crannog was a basically artificial island, usually with a timber and brushwood foundation, supporting a house with a log floor and clay or stone hearth, possibly surrounded by a stockade and with a gangway to the shore. Boulders in or on the structure were seen as providing strength for the uprights or acting as a barrier to water erosion.

THE CONTRIBUTION OF ROBERT MUNRO TO CRANNOG RESEARCH

The most systematic research on the subject of lake-dwellings was carried out by Dr Robert Munro in the last quarter of the nineteenth century. Munro's output was prolific and he excavated and examined many Scottish crannogs and travelled widely studying pile-dwellings of all sorts. The results of his work were published as papers in a wide variety of journals and collected in two major publications, *Ancient Scottish Lake Dwellings*, 1882, and *Lake Dwellings of Europe*, 1890 and he also published major works on other aspects of archaeology.

The major part of *Ancient Scottish Lake Dwellings* consists of the results of the excavation of three Ayrshire crannogs, discovered on the farms of Lochlee, Lochspouts and Buston. These excavations were notable in that they supplied the first reasoned plans and sections of crannogs *(11)*. The excavations were not

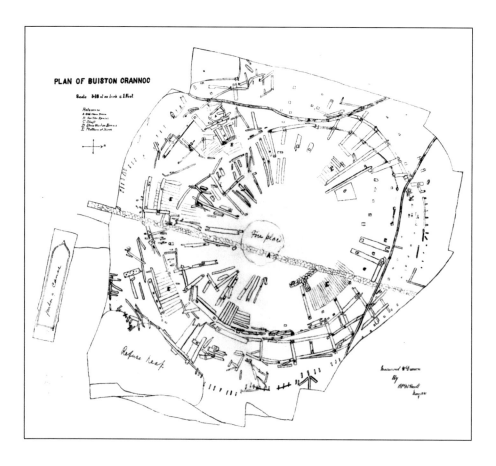

11 Opposite Plan of Buston crannog based on 1879 excavation. *After Munro*

12 Right Decorated wooden plaque from 1879 Buston Crannog excavation. *After Munro*

carried out in a manner acceptable to modern archaeological standards, a point which is clearly established by reference to Munro's own records, but he was well ahead of most other researchers for his time.

The finds from the crannogs which he examined showed Munro a picture of people who practised farming, both crop-cultivation and stock-rearing, supplemented by hunting, fishing, shellfish and wild-fruit gathering. Finds also displayed a wide range of industries including: metalworking in the form of crucibles and moulds; spinning and weaving in the form of spindle-whorls and loom-weights; milling by querns to process the grain; and fishing as seen by net-weights and hooks.

Less industrial pastimes were displayed in decorative and ornamental objects such as bracelets, necklaces, rings and beads and artistic motifs are represented on these and other finds like bone combs and a carved wooden plaque from Buston Crannog *(12)*.

During the period when Munro was carrying out his work on crannogs and lake-dwellings other notices were also published ranging in location from the island of Mull in the Inner Hebrides (Campbell 1870, 465) to Loch Hogsetter on the island of Whalsey in the Shetlands (Mitchell 1881, 303-15). Usually these were no more than descriptions and the observers could add little or nothing to the general concepts put forward by Munro.

His involvement with crannogs brought him into the front line of the controversy, which arose in the final years of the nineteenth and the first few years of the twentieth centuries, over the finds discovered on three sites in the Clyde Estuary – crannogs at Dumbuck, Langbank and at the nearby dun of Dunbuie. All three sites produced material which would fit acceptably an Iron Age date but another group of material of slate and sandstone was so unusual as to defy classification.

Munro and other eminent archaeologists denounced these latter finds as fakes but the controversy lasted for years with the excavators and their supporters attempting to assign the material to a Neolithic phase. Munro's arguments were clear and cogent and resulted in the publication of a book entitled *Archaeology and False Antiquities* (1905). He did not ignore the importance of the estuarine structures although he was unable to classify them as dwellings, beacons or watchtowers. He saw them as representative of a few such sites found in an estuarine situation such as that visited by him on the island of Eriskay (Munro 1885). Recent doctoral research by Alex Hale, when he was a student at Edinburgh University, is helping to clarify the situation of marine crannogs. The impact of Munro's work upon the subject of crannogs was considerable and has survived until the present time. In fact, he was so commanding in the field that his construction sequences, right or wrong, have survived until today and are still trotted out by archaeologists who mention crannogs in their books but know little about them.

During the twentieth century until his death in 1920 Munro published works on a wide variety of subjects and although he never relinquished his interest in crannogs; in later life he was less involved than in earlier years.

REV. F.O. BLUNDELL, THE FIRST
UNDERWATER ARCHAEOLOGIST IN SCOTLAND

In the first 15 years of the twentieth century, a number of the artificial islands in the Highland area were examined by a remarkable priest, Rev. F.O. Blundell of St Benedict's Abbey, Fort Augustus. His work was eventually carried out under the auspices of a committee of the British Association which included Robert Munro among its members.

In 1908, Blundell, for his own interest, examined two sites in a bay at the west end of Loch Ness (Blundell 1909, 159-64). Eilean nan Con, the smaller of the two, is underwater due to the raising of the loch by 2m after the construction of the Caledonian Canal in the nineteenth century. Blundell thought it to be a natural island as its proximity to the shore would offer little protection and he could detect no 'artificial material' about it. On a visit to the site in 1986 bedrock was observed on the site supporting his belief that it was natural. He saw Eilean Muireach, or Cherry Island, as a more interesting proposition and examined it by means of a diving suit borrowed from the Clyde Navigation Trust.

At Blundell's instigation a Committee of the British Association was formed to 'investigate and ascertain the distribution' of crannogs in the Highlands. While he continued his personal examinations a circular was sent to many of the Highland clergy and landowners asking for information regarding sites in their parishes or on their property. From the replies more than fifty new references were added to the list made available by Munro and the earlier workers and he published them in PSAS between 1908 and 1913.

Finance was ultimately obtained with the aim of excavating one of the sites, an island in the Loch of Kinellan, but before the work could commence Blundell left for the Continent as a chaplain with the British forces in the First World War where he saw action in the Battle of Jutland. The site was excavated but not very effectively. After the war Blundell did not go back to his crannog researches but carried out many good works with the poor in Liverpool before his death in 1945. His work had resulted in observations and descriptions of a number of sites and established that large numbers of crannogs were to be found in the Highlands, not only in the south-west as Munro's work had tended to suggest.

The withdrawal of Blundell from the scene and finally the death of Robert Munro in 1920 saw the effective end of serious lake-dwelling studies in Scotland until the 1970s. Five sites were excavated in the intervening period with a wide range of variable results but with little coherent interpretation to assist the creation of crannog classifications.

Six

CRANNOG EXCAVATIONS IN THE TWENTIETH CENTURY

THE LOCH OF KINELLAN

The site that had been chosen for excavation by Odo Blundell was an island in the Loch of Kinellan, near Strathpeffer *(colour plate 2)*, and it was duly excavated by Mr Hugh Fraser, a teacher from Dingwall Academy, in place of Blundell (Fraser 1917).

The excavation was unsatisfactory, albeit with on-the-spot advice by Robert Munro. Fraser's strategy of digging numerous small pits on the surface of the island allowed no large-scale plans of even the upper structures and made it impossible to associate elements of different features. He was forced to excavate in this manner because the island was still surrounded by water which flooded the pits at varying depths of between 1-1.5m below the surface of the island and the timbers of the substructure were reached around 3m below the autumn water level.

The island in the Loch of Kinellan covers half-an-acre and, according to the results of excavation in 1915, was constructed in the same manner as the crannogs in the south-west with a timber framework and a substantial build-up of organic debris, large worked and unworked timbers, layers of peat, mortice joints and hearths. These and the remains of habitation debris in the form of parched barley, ash, bones, hazelnuts and leaves pointed to large amounts of structural and cultural evidence. That it was a multi-phase site was indicated by a layer showing evidence of abandonment between upper and lower occupation phases. The upper part of the site was apparently Medieval in date, according to finds of glazed pottery in abundance, but 'small pieces of fired clay' and 'fragments of pottery' at the base of one of the pits around 3m below the surface may indicate daub and less well-made pottery of an earlier type.

Nineteen pits were dug in all as it was not possible to cut large trenches due to the ingress of water and even the pits were affected by this problem. He referred to the difficulties of encroaching water eight times in his paper to the Inverness Scientific Society and recounted the efforts which he made to combat them. The pits were made deliberately small and, in some cases where pits were enlarged, the part which had already been examined was backfilled so that there was less area through which water could percolate. Fraser constructed a home-made water pump from bicycle tyre inner tubing and tin cans to try and keep the excavations clear but with little success and eventually he had to abandon the early trenches.

The potential of the site was not realised, mainly as a result of the excavation strategy dictated by the water problem. No site plan was produced although all 19 pits showed clear evidence of many timber features. It was not even possible to establish how many houses the island had supported or whether they were circular or rectangular. The lack of analysis of the mass of environmental material and the impossibility of dating the site except from the finds meant that little could be said about the people who lived there in the early periods.

LOCHEND LOCH, COATBRIDGE

In 1932, Lochend Loch, Coatbridge, was drained for cleaning and deepening. An oval crannog, measuring approximately 36m x 27m emerged some 21m from the shore. The site was excavated by workmen under the supervision of Mr Ludovic Mann and reported in PSAS by James Monteith (1937, 26-43). The remains of a central living area constructed of horizontal timbers was uncovered close to a number of vertical piles. Evidence of habitation was seen in the form of worked wood, stone discs, an upper quernstone, a portion of a jet bracelet and a group of coarse pottery characteristic of prehistoric material. A wooden 'shoe' to support a vertical post had been pegged to the clay floor of the second habitation phase.

The site was very muddy and a water pump was used much of the time to keep the trenches relatively dry. Although the standards of excavation were not up to the level required in modern archaeology, a plan and two sections were published. This is one of the only crannogs where human bones were found. The fragments of two skeletons were uncovered. One, from the inside of the house, had been burnt and the other, from 'outside the boundary' had not. The latter showed evidence of a healed fracture of the left leg. No conclusions were reached as to the date of the site or to the economy and history of its inhabitants.

The potential for useful information about the structure and the inhabitants was high as the floor area had uprights still set into mortices in the horizontal timbers. At least two floor levels were excavated and coarse pottery suggests that the early phases may have been of prehistoric date. The description of a small vessel sounds like a crucible suggesting on-site metalworking. Many pieces of worked wood may be in some cases the remains of furniture, according to Monteith, and a wooden post-base in a circle of beams surrounding a stone floor was possibly the pivot for a door. Cattle teeth and hazelnuts are the only evidence of foodstuffs and the excavator suggested that the hazelnuts may have been ground on a rotary quern the remains of which were discovered. The dwelling was apparently burnt down leaving the remains of the two human skeletons.

The loch was drained prior to excavation but most of the work was carried out in very muddy conditions and a commercial water pump was used to keep the site dry. The mud or 'peat soup' was shovelled into barrows by workmen and then taken along slippery planks to the shore. As in the Loch of Kinellan, the pump was continually clogged by peat and wood but Monteith recorded, 'I may say that we could not have worked in this area at all had we not had the use of the petrol pump ...' (Monteith 1937, 28). The 'peat' overlying the floors was treated as spoil. There is no evidence in the report that it was considered as habitation debris and it was not analysed. The site was only partially excavated since the local council who owned the loch wanted to refill it. The site is now in the public park at Monkton and it is likely that there is still evidence under the waters of the park pond.

LOCH TREIG, INVERNESS-SHIRE

In 1933 Professor James Ritchie of Edinburgh University was informed that a crannog in Loch Treig, Inverness-shire was exposed above the water level which had been lowered substantially while the loch was dammed to supply water for the British Aluminium Company Works in Fort William. He organised and supervised excavations on the site in July of that year (Ritchie 1942, 8-78).

The superficially stony mound was discovered to have a core consisting substantially of layers of timbers, brushwood, peat, earth and stones. A great number of horizontal timbers were uncovered representing an upper living platform and underlying foundation structure with relatively few vertical piles compared to other excavated crannogs.

Professor Ritchie considered the site to be of a distinctive and developed construction with features analogous to other Scottish and Irish sites but with more differences than similarities. The few finds from the site are from unclear contexts. Insofar as they indicate any date for habitation it would be from the Medieval period, as late as the sixteenth or seventeenth centuries AD in the final phase. This speculation is not surprising as there are references to it being occupied at that time. Remains of a shoe were assigned 'later than 500 AD' and Ritchie thought it likely that the Loch Treig crannog-builders lived at the end of, or soon after, Romano-British times. Further excavation for clearly associated timbers would help to clarify the situation with radiocarbon dates.

Excavation was carried out in the usual method by a team of workmen under the supervision of an archaeologist. Although a lengthy report was produced (Ritchie 1942) it dealt almost exclusively with a detailed description and reconstruction of the timber structure to a level which could hardly be justified by the extent of the excavation. Pits were opened in the top of the mound and sections were cut near the outside edges but it appears from the plates in the excavator's report that a clear and concise outline of the structure as portrayed in the record could not have been realised.

He reconstructed the dwelling as a rectangular house on a similar substructure but the mound as it stands is almost circular. He inferred that the upper platform had been constructed in such a way as to be always submerged and outlined an ingenious method by which the builders lowered the level of the loch so that they could construct the island in dry conditions.

The site was dated to the sixteenth century AD by these finds but the depths of organic debris and the layers observed during excavation may suggest a number of phases of rebuilding over a lengthy period of time. The layers of peat and heather were construed as building materials and were apparently not examined for evidence of habitation.

One discrepancy in the report was observed during a visit to the site in 1983 as the crannog was exposed by the low level of the loch *(13)*. A ridge of material with substantial longitudinal timbers suggested evidence consistent with a gangway to the shore although Ritchie stated that he had observed no such timbers even after cutting trenches along and across the ridge. The 1983 visit, motivated by the report of a very low loch level, showed that the mound is still very substantial with a number of large timbers projecting from the sides. It would be possible to acquire samples from these timbers for radiocarbon dates from different levels of the site.

It is also recorded, in the records of the North of Scotland Hydro-Electric Board archives, that Professor Ritchie examined a crannog in Loch Garry which was exposed when the water level in the loch was lowered for hydro-electric power related work but, unfortunately, he died before publishing the results of that work.

13 Keppoch's Council Isle, Loch Treig, photographed in 1986 when loch level was particularly low. *N. Dixon*

MILTON LOCH CRANNOG I, KIRKCUDBRIGHT

The 1940s saw the substantial excavations carried out by Hencken at Lagore and Balinderry in Ireland (Hencken 1937, 1942, 1950) but no more work was carried out in Scotland until 1950 when one of two crannogs discovered in Milton Loch, Kirkcudbright was excavated by C.M. Piggott (Piggott 1953). This excavation is the closest published report to the standards required of modern archaeology, and yet conclusions were reached by the excavator, particularly in regard to chronology, which were later proved wrong. Milton Loch was not a total excavation as the base of the site was always below water level, more so as the work proceeded, and the level rose during the course of the excavation.

More than 300 upright posts and piles and substantial arrays of horizontal beams at Milton Loch represented the plan and floor layout of a prehistoric house. Two boulder areas outlined by piles represented the remains of breakwaters enclosing a harbour. The area they covered was as large as that covered by the house and platform (Piggott 1953, fig. 2) and may therefore be considered an important element of the site. Clear evidence of a timber gangway leading from the shore to the dwelling place gave an alternative to canoes or boats for access.

Few finds came from Milton Loch Crannog but those that did were instructive and, in one case, misleading. A fragment of a quernstone in conjunction with cereal and weeds of cultivation pollen are enough to show that arable farming was being practised, but more vivid still was the discovery of the head and stilt of an early ard, a sort of rudimentary plough (Piggott 1953, 143).

The construction of the crannog was dated to the second century AD according to the discovery of a bronze loop dress-fastener with Pannonian features and a presumably Roman auxiliary origin. About 15 years after the excavation, a radiocarbon date of 400±100 BC (K-1394. Lerche 1969) was obtained for the ard parts. It was considered too early because such sophisticated ploughs were not at that time considered relevant to a second-century AD date, much less to a period some 700 years earlier. However, another timber sample from the site was dated in 1973 and supplied a date closely similar to that taken from the ard (490±100 BC K-2027. Guido 1974, 54).

This discovery significantly altered the conclusions reached by Mrs Piggott in the 1953 report. Assuming that the dress fastener was a stratified find from occupation layers, and not just a single lost object, the site must have had at least two phases of occupation with construction in the Early Iron Age.

It is notable that there was no overburden of large boulders and above the wooden floor were 'small weathered stones and plant roots' (Piggott 1953, 136). The excavator makes no comment about the layer of humic material which is clearly seen in one of the site photographs and this may be partly the remains of habitation debris which had built-up during occupation of the site. The floorboards beneath this overburden were flat on top but rounded on the bottom, like those seen at Oakbank Crannog in Loch Tay (see below). These were probably the subject of considerable erosion on top rather than deliberate cutting. This evidence would suggest either that the site had been abandoned for a length of time with these timbers exposed and was then reoccupied, or that the floor was in use long enough for this erosion to have taken place.

The upper area of the crannog was almost all exposed during excavation and a plan of the horizontal timbers and piles allowed the excavator to produce an outline plan and reconstruction of the house and surrounding walkway with a reasonable level of confidence. The bronze loop dress-fastener dating to the second century AD and the ard-stilt dating to the fifth century BC suggest at least two periods of occupation so far apart in time that some reconstruction must have taken place in the later phase. The massive number of piles surrounding the island were randomly distributed according to Piggott but this is unlikely and the apparently haphazard arrangement is likely to be a result of the different phases of building and strengthening represented by the uprights.

For the first time in a crannog excavation seeds from a recognisably functional feature, the hearth, were examined and a sample of peat was analysed for pollen. Polygonum was well represented both in the peat and from the hearth; it is a plant not only found in conjunction with cereal but gathered in its own right as a food source (Renfrew 1973, 183). Grass and a wide variety of herbaceous pollens were recognised, many of them weeds of cultivation. Cereal pollen was also discovered and together with the ard-stilt and a rotary quernstone, shows good evidence for arable farming.

Similar types of pollen and seeds and an ard from Oakbank Crannog indicate an economy in essence the same as at Milton Loch (see below). In fact, although the latter is slightly smaller overall than Oakbank Crannog, the two sites are similar in a number of ways. Both have the remains of pile-supported gangways to the shore and remains of either a jetty or harbour; timber-floor layers of complete trunks eroded on the top; clear evidence of arable agriculture including remains of ards; and a mass of surrounding piles representing more than one phase of occupation. Phases of both sites are seen to be contemporary by radiocarbon dating. Piggott was of the opinion that highland and lowland crannogs were 'basically different' and that the latter supported more permanent habitation. She also thought the lowland sites were on the whole earlier although she said it was not possible to claim a difference in date between the two groups.

The upper foundation layers immediately underneath the floor at Milton Loch Crannog were exposed but the lower foundation structure was below the water and it was not possible to examine it or establish whether lower floors existed. The excavator stated in the report that the ard was 'almost certainly deposited deliberately beneath the house foundations as a ritual offering to the gods ...' (Piggott 1953, 144), presumably under the impression that there was only one floor and that the ard could not have been deposited beneath it in any other way. Doubt must be introduced to this theory, given the date of the ard and the fact that the Pannonian-type loop-fastener was found on the floor, but it is notable that the Oakbank ard was also directly beneath the upper floor there. This does not necessarily imply support for a theory of ritual deposition since wooden ards may not have been of great value and therefore removed upon abandonment of a site and would be left lying on the top of the habitation debris build-up to be directly overlain by subsequent floors.

LOCH GLASHAN, ARGYLLSHIRE

In April 1960 the waters of Loch Glashan, Argyll were lowered by 4m in the course of work on a hydro-electric scheme. Some 3m below the former water level, close to a small natural island in the south-east section of the loch, lay the remains of a crannog. The exposed areas of the site were excavated by Mr J.G. Scott of Glasgow Art Gallery and Museum, reported in *Discovery and Excavation in Scotland*, 1960 (DES 1960, 8-9). The depth of water over the site suggested that the water level had risen considerably after abandonment. It was an oval, stone-covered mound 17m x 11m prior to excavation but removal of the stones exposed a substantially timber structure.

Observation suggested that the foundations of the crannog were brushwood lying on the mud of the loch bed, in some cases overlain with oak or silver-birch logs. Some piles were seen at the edge of the crannog furthest from the shore but there is no record of the number. The DES report states:

> The stones proved to be a thin scatter, except in the northwest sector, where they were some 3 feet deep, perhaps marking the site of a round hut, about 12 feet in diameter. This building appeared to be later than a rectangular structure, about 25 feet by 15 feet in size, defined by a series of massive, parallel oak timbers, their tops in some cases flattened, suggesting the floor of a house.
> (*Scott 1960, 8-9*)

It is possible that the 'rectangular structure' was the remains of the flooring of a rectangular or circular house in the form of a 'platform' as demonstrated in other crannog excavations (Milton Loch, Buston, etc.). The 'flattened tops' of some of the floor timbers may have been caused by water erosion rather than deliberate attempts by the crannog-dwellers to produce a flat floor. The same effect is seen at Oakbank Crannog, Loch Tay (see below).

Organic finds from Loch Glashan were represented by well-preserved wooden objects: 'A trough, four trough-like bowls, a paddle, a scoop, several worked timbers of a structural kind and numerous pegs and pins.' The wooden finds have recently been re-examined with interesting results (Earwood 1990). There were also remains of a number of leather objects '... including parts of sheaths, shoes, and of a jerkin'. Evidence of crop cultivation may be postulated by the discovery of 20 quernstones on the site at least some of which must have been for grinding grain. A bronze penannular brooch and Dark Age E ware pottery, suggest a date in the seventh to ninth centuries AD for at least part of the occupation of the site but, recalling the case of Milton Loch Crannog, original construction may have been substantially earlier. The excavator recorded: 'There were some indications of the posts of an older structure lying beneath the other two, but, since this was below the water level at the time, it could not be investigated.'

LATER SURVEYS

Since 1960 occasional notices of crannogs have been included in field surveys (for example Campbell and Sandeman 1964, 61). Other work included a final-year dissertation by a student of Edinburgh University, outlining the Scottish evidence (Savory 1971) and a more extensive thesis submitted for an MPhil degree in Archaeology by G. Oakley at Newcastle University in 1973 (Oakley 1973). The latter work is a good summary of the past work and includes a comprehensive bibliography and site gazetteer. In 1973 archaeologists from Edinburgh University in conjunction with a team of Naval Air Command Sub-Aqua Club divers carried out a survey of Loch Awe to establish the number and form of artificial islands in the loch. Possible sites were noted from aerial photographs, Ordnance Survey maps and old references prior to the fieldwork and 20 were eventually confirmed.

Seven

PROBLEMS IN INTERPRETATION

The previous chapters show that a great deal of work was carried out in the past on the subject of Scottish crannogs particularly in the second half of the nineteenth century and the first two decades of the twentieth. Many general surveys and observations were recorded in the south-west of the country and others were examined in the Highlands. Excavations were carried out mainly by Robert Munro in the nineteenth century and occasionally by a number of excavators throughout the twentieth century when the opportunity arose. It might have been expected that such a large effort would have produced a range of comprehensive statements applicable to the construction techniques and structure of the sites and the economy, industrial activities and way of life of their inhabitants; in fact the great majority of these records are merely descriptive accounts which add little in terms of cultural insight into the crannogs or their inhabitants.

Robert Munro was the only archaeologist who attempted to consider crannogs with any deeper insight but in 1882 he expressed doubt that the time was right:

> Notwithstanding the variety and number of objects found in these remains, and the copiousness of details with which the investigations are described, it may still be doubted whether the time has arrived for applying to them the rigid principles of induction, with the view of materially enlarging our knowledge of the early inhabitants of this country. (*Munro 1882, 240*)

His decision to go ahead and make certain inferences was tempered by reservations with regard to his own lack of experience and archaeological abilities:

> In attempting, therefore, to deal with the scientific aspect of these discoveries, I do not for a moment profess such a minute acquaintance with the science of archaeology as to entitle me even to attempt a full exposition of the inferences that may be derived from their careful study and comparison with other antiquarian remains... (*Munro 1882, 241*)

He saw no distinction between the utilisation of natural islands where available and both stone and timber crannogs and thought it reasonable to infer that artificial islands were only resorted to where natural ones were absent. He saw no evidence to suggest that the three types were not contemporary, neither did he see wood as a necessary structural component but thought that stone crannogs were more likely to be found in larger lochs with a firm gravel bed while timber was essential as a foundation material on muddy bottoms. Munro inferred that stone buildings had greater advantages than wooden ones and that they were a natural progression from the crannogs, culminating in moated Medieval castles.

The distribution of crannogs, according to Munro, was restricted to the 'districts formerly occupied by Celtic races' with the majority in the south-west and fewer to the north in the area of the Picts and the Scots. He made the ambiguous statement:

> Nor is this generalisation much affected by an extension of the list, so as to include those stony islets so frequently met with in the Highland lakes. (*Munro 1882, 249*)

These 'stony islets' he had earlier described as '... mere shapeless cairns, without any indications of having been formerly inhabited', but he does not suggest an alternative function for them. In fact, the evidence from Oakbank Crannog shows a site that is effectively the same as Milton Loch Crannog in structure and function and therefore the same as his classic crannog-type from the south-west, at least in their original form. The inclusion of the Highland crannogs in the archaeological record does indeed make a significant difference to the overall distribution of artificial islands but Munro's assertion that 'proper' crannogs were concentrated in the south-west became so well accepted that it has lasted until the present time.

With regard to the structure of crannogs, Munro reiterated the sequence noted by earlier observers of brushwood and logs overlain by stones and earth surrounded by one or more rows of piles. With reference to his excavations of Buston, Lochlee and Lochspouts crannogs in Ayrshire he praised the skills of the crannog-builders:

... all the wooden islands were constructed after one uniform plan, this
plan was actually the outcome of the highest mechanical principles that
the circumstances could admit of. (*Munro 1882, 261*)

and he formulated a more detailed description of the method of construction
consisting of six major elements.

His theory was that a circular raft of logs was positioned above a foundation
deposit of branches and brushwood and was then covered with more timbers
as well as stones and gravel until the mass rested on the loch bed. Ready-cut
oak piles were then inserted through holes in the structure 'and probably also
a few were inserted into the bed of the lake' (Munro 1882, 262). The logs in
the raft were occasionally pinned together by thick oak pegs and the uprights
were fixed with morticed oak beams while other beams were morticed
together to give lateral strength at various levels. When the mass of material
extended above the water level the oak piles which surrounded it were joined
with more morticed beams and a 'prepared pavement of oak-beams was
constructed'. Munro added, 'The margin of the island was also slantingly
shaped by an intricate arrangement of beams and stones ...' producing a well-
formed breakwater. He suggested that turfs were laid over the protruding
points of piles and that '... a superficial barrier of hurdles, or some such fence
...' was erected close to the edge. He also postulated the frequent erection of
a submerged wooden gangway giving secret access to the site. Because of the
lack of evidence for superstructure elements he made no mention of the type
of dwelling or shelters which may have surmounted the pavement.

The inhabitants of the crannogs were, according to Munro, ultimately
descended from European Celts who had constructed the lake-dwellings in
Switzerland and elsewhere on the Continent. These people had migrated to
Britain, because of pressure and conflict in their own lands which resulted
in the abandonment of the lake-dwellings there, and had been driven to the
far north and west by 'successive waves of immigrants'. Their occupation
of the crannogs coincided with the Roman presence in the south-west of
Scotland and the crannogs were built as a response to the times when the
Romans withdrew and left the provincial population to the mercies of their
less civilised neighbours to the north. The close connection, which Munro
proposed between the crannog-builders of Scotland and the lake-dwellers
of Switzerland, was based mainly on the similarities of the two types of site
and he was not in a position at the time of his researches to know that there
were in fact few points of comparison either chronologically or structurally
between the two.

He proposed three reasons for the submergence of crannogs: compaction of
the structural material of the site; sinking into soft bottom muds or general

compression; and sinking of the loch-bed sediments. He suggested that the latter process was the most evident. He did not see water level changes as significant. His conclusions were derived from the results of the excavations which he carried out in the south-west. However, work in Loch Tay (see below) shows that the reasons for submergence of sites there are not in accordance with Munro's statements.

The conclusions arrived at by Munro in *Ancient Scottish Lake Dwellings* have been covered here in some depth since they still represent, for many, the core of crannog thinking. Although he stated his reservations before making inferences at that time, he did not significantly alter his views in his later work.

The high standard of Munro's work for his day is demonstrated by its endurance to the present time and contrasts with the lack of lasting impact of the subject itself. Crannogs are usually treated in a cursory manner by archaeo-logical writers but where they are referred to, it is in the terms laid out by Munro. His structural sequence has not been superseded and the concentration of the distribution of sites in the south-west of Scotland is still accepted. Although archaeological evidence does not now support the notion of crannog-builders originating from the Continental lake-dwellers no other hypothesis has yet replaced Munro's, and although they are no longer restricted chronologically to the post-Roman period, as stated by Munro, the earlier dates now available have not yet become firmly fixed in the archaeological record although recent contributors are changing that view (Barber and Crone 1993, Henderson 1998). Munro's ideas have been so firmly established that they can only be replaced by systematic studies carried out in a chronological and cultural framework not available to him and excavations underwater such as that being carried out at Oakbank Crannog in Loch Tay.

INADEQUACIES OF PAST WORK

Neither Munro and his contemporaries nor the later excavators produced the level of interpretation of either the structure of artificial islands and the dwellings upon them or the way of life of their inhabitants that would be expected now, considering the wealth of well-preserved organic material that was uncovered. This is not a reflection upon the skill of the archaeologists who, given the constraints which applied when they were working, carried out their excavations to an acceptable standard and, in the case of Munro, to a higher standard than was normal for the time.

His structural sequence was so convincing that it has been accepted apparently without question to the present day. However, a number of points are not clear. For instance, how would the layers of brushwood, earth or peat be deposited effectively underwater since the brushwood would float and earth

14 Detail of Lochlee Crannog showing skilled joinery. *After Munro*

would dissipate or change into mud if dropped into any reasonable depth of water? Peat could only be laid in cut blocks but there is no evidence, according to excavation reports, of peat in that form. It may reasonably be argued that these deposits were built up in a less systematic manner, probably above water as floor covering and evidence presented below from Oakbank Crannog supports this theory.

Munro did not explain why the sites were not built as free-standing pile-dwellings since he demonstrated in his excavations, of Buston and Lochlee Crannogs in particular, that the walkways surrounding the sites were skillfully constructed of jointed piles and beams in this way *(14)*. In fact, Munro seems to have been the only archaeologist to ask why the crannog-builders built their sites by dumping layers of material into the water and he gave the answer that the bases of the lochs were too soft and yielding to support true pile-dwellings. If this were the case, then the same reason would prevent the well-morticed pile construction of the surrounding platforms. None of the twentieth-century excavators was in a position to challenge Munro's sequence since in no case did they carry out complete excavation, usually because the bottom of the site was still underwater or was heavily waterlogged.

Most of the past work on crannogs emphasised the structural elements of the island itself, understandably, since most of it would have been permanently underwater and therefore better preserved than the actual house which was always intended to be above the surface. However, features of the dwelling were preserved and have been recognised in most of the excavations. Log pavements or platforms usually constructed of small unworked tree-trunks were common and were often associated with one or more hearths. Some of the piles surrounding the site and other timbers nearer the centre probably represented remains of the house exterior walls, supports for the roof and internal partitions.

Munro said nothing about the form of the houses that stood on the crannogs which he excavated. Reconstructions were attempted by Professor Ritchie with regard to the crannog in Loch Treig and Mrs Piggott for Milton Loch crannog. The first of these was highly speculative as it was based on evidence mainly from the substructure which was itself conjectural and was not completely uncovered. The Milton Loch house is also speculative but at least the upper layers were uncovered and the plan is based on observed uprights and floor timbers.

There is no record of efforts by past workers to delineate the area of the house and the boundaries of specific activity areas. It would have been more difficult to do so if the material overlying the floors which contained debris indicative of industrial and domestic functions was treated as spoil, which it usually was. The number of hearths was often recorded and their vertical distribution was also occasionally noted but there is seldom an accurate record of their association with other features and with each other.

The dates assigned to crannogs in the days prior to the development of radiocarbon or dendrochronological techniques were based on the evidence of finds and in most cases fell between the time of the Roman occupation and the Medieval period. Munro was adamant in his assertion that no crannog which had been examined was earlier than the Roman Iron Age (Munro 1886, 465). Piggott was of the opinion that Milton Loch Crannog was built and inhabited in the second century AD but was proved to be some 700 years too late by radiocarbon dates. It is reasonable to accept the dates based on finds assigned by early researchers as relating to phases of occupation, at which time the particular find was deposited, but many sites may have been occupied a number of times and the first structural phase cannot be assigned by finds unless they are unambiguously associated with that phase. It is notable that the great majority of radiocarbon dates from crannogs, so far, fall in the first millennium BC and a number as early as the eighth century BC (Henderson 1998).

It can be seen from the summary of past results that emphasis was placed on study of the structural timbers, mainly from foundation layers, and surrounding piles and stakes. Where the lower foundation deposits were underwater greater emphasis was placed on upper foundation layers and the remains of floors. Very little was said about the crannog-builders and dwellers or about the details of houses and internal features even though a mass of data was lying on and under the floors in the form of organic debris. It will be shown in the report and summary of the excavations being carried out on Oakbank Crannog, Loch Tay that these and broader aspects of crannog work can be successfully studied through excavation, analysis and interpretation using modern methods and techniques which were not available to the early archaeologists.

THE PROBLEMS OF PAST EXCAVATIONS

One of the main problems with early crannog research was the method of excavation. Usually a gang of workmen were employed to shovel the spoil from the site into barrows and dump it on nearby spoil-heaps. The work was supervised and observed by the archaeologist who would make sketches of what he considered were important features. If he was not on site at all times he would examine the spoil heaps and any finds that the workmen had picked up upon his return. This method of working would have serious consequences for the number and range of finds discovered but more importantly the context and association of finds and features would in many, if not most, cases be lost.

The inadequacy of such methods would be particularly severe on a crannog where many of the features are constructed of soft timbers which can easily be cut through with a spade. An imbalance would be created in the types of wood recognised in structures since oak would not be cut or broken while other types would be easily destroyed. Robert Munro was one of the most conscientious excavators in the nineteenth century and records sieving the spoil from Buston crannog but this was obviously not wholly effective as he discusses elsewhere cases where finds were discovered later having been removed from the site during the excavation. An ancient forgery of a Saxon coin was found in material removed from the site by a local schoolteacher. It was brought to the attention of Munro, but many other finds must have been dispersed without record such as a number of objects 'publicly exhibited at a bazaar in Kilmarnock'.

Another aspect of the early methods of excavation, which would inhibit efficient study, was the habit of digging pits into the top of the site or opening small trenches. The problem has been discussed already in relation to the excavations at the Loch of Kinellan. This practice in conjunction with the problem of using untrained workmen must make the results from many of the early sites of dubious accuracy.

Accurate recording of features in the form of measured plans and sections was not carried out on many sites and even where it was the results were often at a scale too small to be of much use. Not only does this mean that there were few plans for future research and comparison, but with the complex arrangements of timbers and layers on a crannog the excavator would not be able to retain them all in his memory and site interpretation must have suffered. Usually only areas which seemed to be of particular structural interest to the excavator were sketched so that records of the site are highly subjective. This same problem of subjectivity was practised with regard to finds in that attractive artefacts were collected for museum or personal display but the many unassuming wooden objects which must have been uncovered on crannogs were hardly mentioned.

DISADVANTAGES OF DRAINED SITES

The single major problem which has done most to prevent the systematic study of crannogs and has caused the greatest difficulties with the work that has been carried out is that of waterlogging. Crannogs by definition are built in water and their remains are still in or under water. Although some efforts have been made to examine sites which are still islands the difficulties which these endeavours encountered are demonstrated by the work carried out in the Loch of Kinellan. Even sites which were substantially drained but where the lower layers were still submerged, as in the cases of Milton Loch Crannog and the site in Loch Glashan, could not be excavated completely.

Total drainage has usually been accepted as the best method, until recently the only method, of approaching excavation of an artificial island. However, working on a drained site is very much a compromise as there are many problems associated with drainage. The cost of damming a site is very expensive and would probably not be seen as justifiable for archaeological research. The cost of damming a number of crannogs which would be required for systematic studies would be prohibitive.

In past work the sites have been drained for other purposes, mainly agricultural in the nineteenth century and hydro-electric power schemes in the twentieth. The later excavations have often been restricted in time by the necessity to re-flood the loch and could not guarantee a fully drained site. Furthermore, since there was no question of choice of site the work could not be systematic or prepared for. Even sites which were totally drained, such as Lochlee which had been dry for 40 years before Munro excavated it, were in areas with a high water table and suffered from water leaking into the low levels of the excavation. Munro's records of the excavations at Lochlee, Buston, Lochspouts, Barhapple and Friar's Carse make up the greater part of his book, *Ancient Scottish Lake Dwellings*, on which so much has been based. Yet he talks in every case of work being curtailed to one extent or another because of water.

It would be difficult to observe fine or subtle features in the unavoidable muds of a drained, but still wet, crannog and small finds such as pins and beads would not be easy to see. All of the objects from the excavation would have to be washed clean to establish the degree of working and cut-marks of tools, if any. None of the past excavators record carrying out such a task and it would seem inevitable that a large number of small finds and features were missed.

The decay of organic deposits starts within minutes of exposure, even underwater, as was demonstrated during the excavation of Oakbank Crannog (see below). Thus, the effect of draining a site must be the loss of a great deal of archaeologically important material. Damage caused subsequently by wind, rain and sun would be enormous. The deposits which have been drained are thus necessarily in a worse state of decay than if they had remained beneath the water surface.

Decay is not the only danger to organic objects on a drained site, as mechanical damage would have been far greater than when the object was underwater. Thin pieces of wood and material like basketwork would not in their weakened state support their own weight so the chance of successful exposure and removal of many finds would be slight. One of the most severe causes of mechanical damage may be illustrated by the results of a simple experiment. A number of timbers from Oakbank Crannog were weighed underwater with a spring balance. The total weight was 1.36kg. The same timbers weighed out of the water totalled 14kg, an increase of more than tenfold.

The implications of this may be more fully appreciated by looking at the photographs of Milton Loch Crannog during excavation. The considerable numbers of large timbers express a significantly heavy force upon the archaeo-logical features and artefacts underlying them. This force would only be exerted by bringing the mass of timbers above the surface, at which time damage to delicate archaeological material is inevitable.

Another disadvantage of draining a crannog would be the task of removing timbers during excavation, presuming that they were required to be kept in one piece. A number of people would be required to lift and carry the larger timbers across the slippery, muddy surface of the site. Since a timber weighing 20kg underwater would weigh 200kg in air the potentially disastrous results of a slip by only one of the carriers can be appreciated. Of more concern archaeo-logically is the effect of trampling upon underlying deposits during such an operation and throughout the work of excavation.

There are other disadvantages of carrying out archaeological excavation of crannogs only when they are fortuitously drained for agricultural purposes or exposed for industrial development. It is possible that a site, where continued access relies upon the scheduling of other projects, may not be available long enough for effective examination or excavation to take place. This was the case during the excavation in Lochend Loch when the local council required the site to be reflooded for use as a boating pond.

Crannogs presented in this randomly selected manner may well be in isolated locations, as in the case of Loch Treig, without close association with regional or local groups and although this does not lessen the inherent importance of any site it would be more useful to choose one which might add to established knowledge than to be forced to study an isolated monument. A serious disadvantage of studying unassociated crannogs is that they will only fit into the existing body of knowledge relating to artificial islands in the same haphazard manner that applied to previous excavations. Given the probable impediments to effective study presented above, they are likely to add little more to the archaeological record than those examined in the past.

CHRONOLOGY

Absolute methods of dating archaeological sites, like radiocarbon assay and dendrochronological analysis, were not readily available to crannog excavators prior to the 1960s. Thus, as with other sites, dating was by association of finds which placed crannogs in a range from the Roman Iron Age to the post-Medieval period. Since many crannogs have apparently been reused a number of times, there is no way of dating the primary construction unless the finds were definitely associated with established elements of the original structure. The above difficulties of excavation, observation and recording make it unlikely that such elements were, or could be, established so the finds upon which the loose framework of crannog chronology is based may be from periods of occupation long separated from either the date of construction or other periods of habitation.

A major problem in assimilating the broad range of crannog knowledge into the archaeological record was directly related to the common tradition of examining the record by periods. Since crannogs were dated by artefact association to a number of periods, but did not fit neatly into one, they were occasionally briefly mentioned by archaeologists specialising in the study of a specific period but the greatest effort of these researchers was expended upon site types which were confined chronologically within their particular area of research. Crannogs were neglected and there is no corpus of knowledge developed and established in the same manner as that referring to other types of sites.

Efforts do not seem to have been made in the past to construct relative site chronologies with different phases distinguished by archaeologically distinct features and arrangements of timbers. Munro observed superimposed hearths at Lochlee and Lochspouts; Fraser distinguished upper and lower phases on the island in the Loch of Kinellan and many distinct layers; Scott referred to two separate houses at Loch Glashan and an earlier phase under the water but none of them attempted to define chronologically the length of different phases or the overall period of habitation. The problems of excavating on drained or partially drained sites, particularly in terms of detailed observation and recording difficulties, may be major factors to blame for the lack of definition.

FUTURE RESEARCH

Although a substantial amount of work has been carried out in the past on the subject of crannogs, with relatively systematic study in the nineteenth century and a number of excavation reports from the twentieth, little of substance was added to the archaeological record in Scotland. This is slowly changing with the involvement of other researchers using modern techniques. The most important change which has taken place since the early crannog researches is the progressive development in all aspects of archaeology but in particular, for the problems discussed above, in the standards of excavation. Rigorous observation and recording of context, stratigraphy and association has improved both quantitatively and qualitatively the information derived from these archaeological sites.

The problem of dating has been substantially overcome by the invention and adoption of radiocarbon dating and latterly dendrochronological dating. Both of these techniques require amounts of organic material; small amounts of a wide range of substances in the case of radiocarbon determinations, and discernible tree rings on substantial timbers in the case of dendrochronology and both are therefore applicable to the dating of organic and timber-rich sites like crannogs. As noted above, most radiocarbon dates available so far from crannogs fall in the first millennium BC suggesting that sites already excavated may have been constructed earlier than had been supposed (see below).

One of the most potentially productive associations may be that between the examination and analysis of organic debris from crannogs and the wide range of environmental studies which have become established in the last three decades. Seeds, pollen and macro-plant remains are found on many artificial islands and may also include insect remains, eggs, larvae, snails and excreta from a wide range of organisms. Whereas in past work this mass of material was treated much as spoil it may now be used in various ways: to delineate specific working areas; to indicate the range of plants used for food and the types and level of crops cultivated; to suggest climatic variations; and to chronicle the evolution of the landscape. Sophisticated and well-considered sampling techniques now available make possible the recognition and interpretation of a wide range of naturally and artificially deposited materials from crannogs.

UNDERWATER EXCAVATION TO OVERCOME THE EFFECTS OF DRAINAGE

The problems of crude methodology, inadequate dating and the lack of effective analysis of organic deposits can now be overcome with modern developments in archaeology. The effects of draining a site and the ensuing problems of working it cannot be overcome in archaeological terms. If drainage on demand is too expensive and inadvisable anyway because of the effects listed above, the alternative is to excavate the site underwater in the environment which has already protected it for so long.

The excavation of crannogs underwater with the benefit of modern excavation techniques and standards of recording allows important information to be derived scientifically from these sites. Examination of timbers in situ enables close dating of the sites and recognition of different phases of habitation, while sampling of other organic deposits makes possible accurate studies of climatic changes and the development of the landscape. Many of the problems of excavating crannogs on land do not apply on an underwater excavation.

A submerged site to be excavated may be chosen with regard to the results of pre-excavation survey. Exposed timbers and organic deposits can be readily sampled and analysed for dating and environmental indications before a stone is moved. Since the work is not related to the timetables of industrial development or agricultural land use the imposition of working to a deadline need not apply.

The limited information now available from past excavations is no longer the best that can be expected, although the basis of new research and much of the new work is based upon questions posed by the early researchers. The surveys of Loch Awe in 1973, Loch Tay in 1979 and Loch Lomond in 1997 demonstrate that many crannogs are located relatively close to each other. Where contemporaneity can be proven, as in the case of Oakbank Crannog and a nearby site in Loch Tay, comparisons and contrasts of the material from these sites are very important and ambiguous questions on one site may be answered by work carried out on the other.

More practical problems are also overcome by underwater excavation. The difficulties of observation on a muddy site do not exist as such under water. There is no restriction upon the depth of layers of excavation. The basal layers are as accessible as the upper features and work can also be carried out on the surrounding loch bed where fish traps and canoes may be suspected. The weight of timbers is no threat to delicate finds and archaeological features and they can be easily removed with the minimum of disturbance since the worker under water can float across the site without touching it if need be. Delicate artefacts sustain their own weight underwater and may be moved into storage containers with the minimum of handling.

The removal of spoil is facilitated by a number of tools now available to underwater archaeologists with a great deal less effort than on land and large areas of loch bed are available for convenient dumping. Underwater areas for storage are also available for large finds which are not undergoing immediate conservation in a laboratory.

A major aim of this book is to demonstrate that the underwater excavation of crannogs is feasible, financially viable and archaeologically valuable. The developments in underwater excavation which have made this work possible are outlined, as are the results of underwater surveys in both large and small Scottish lochs, supplying a context for the excavation of Oakbank Crannog. The work carried out there since 1980 and the exciting results are discussed in depth.

Eight

RECENT CRANNOG SURVEYS IN SCOTLAND

Submerged settlement sites were first examined in the nineteenth century and since then they have all been considered under the name 'crannog'. Many people have observed and reported crannogs in the field for more than 150 years but the great majority did not record them with sufficient accuracy for those reports to be of great use to today's researchers. Modern surveys, which started with a survey of Loch Awe in 1973 (McArdle *et al* 1973), are now adding considerably to our understanding of Scotland's artificial islands.

Many of the small islands seen in Scottish lochs are artificial although it is not always obvious. Elements that indicate that an island is man-made include unnatural angles and slopes, homogeneous make-up of large stones and evidence of cut timbers or buildings, although stone and timber buildings could also be found on natural islands. The addition of jetties, boat noosts and small harbours may also indicate artificiality. The best method of searching for crannogs is with aerial photography and now, with modern diving techniques and electronic survey equipment, it is relatively simple to accurately examine and plan crannogs even when they are totally submerged.

Recently, a number of surveys have been carried out in Scotland and a collection of them is described here. The list is necessarily selective but will hopefully give a balanced picture of the sort of remains that are being discovered, spanning many time periods, and also give an indication of the range that is still to be found. The sites looked at over the last 20 years cover the whole of Scotland from the Outer Hebrides in the north to Dumfries and Galloway in the south and from Loch Tollaidh, Ross-shire in the west to Loch Clunie, Perthshire in the east.

One of the first resources to access when considering Scottish lochs is the *Bathymetrical Survey of the Freshwater Lochs of Scotland* produced by Murray and

Pullar in 1910. These two elderly men rowed around 560 of Scotland's lochs in the first decade of the twentieth century taking depth readings and producing very accurate charts from the results. They often recorded on the maps crannogs that they saw on their travels. In the past I have made visits to a number of libraries to access the six volumes of their work but now they can all be consulted on the website of the National Library of Scotland making the task very much simpler.

The methods used to record and plan crannogs varies considerably depending on the state of the site. In some cases they are tree-covered islands and in others completely submerged mounds of stone. Where there are few identifiable features it is often sufficient to use tapes, compasses and measuring staffs to produce an adequate record. Where a site is more complicated, the total station (a very accurate electronic theodolite) is used when the expensive machine sits safely on the shore and the prism that reflects the beam is mounted on the top of a staff carried by a diver. Plans can be directly logged and the site plan instantly drawn on a laptop computer. Modern global positioning system (GPS) hand-held machines are now relatively cheap and are extremely useful in establishing the position of a submerged site that may otherwise be difficult to relocate in the future. With the equipment available now there is no reason why islands and submerged sites are not included in archaeological area surveys as a matter of fact in the same way that dry land sites are considered.

ARTIFICIAL ISLANDS IN THE OUTER HEBRIDES

In 1985, the first ever underwater survey took place on the Isle of Lewis to establish what sort of artificial islands existed there (Dixon and Topping 1986). There are literally hundreds of island sites in the Outer Hebrides and it is only possible to give a few examples here.

Loch an Duin, Shader (NB 393544)
The site consisted of a stone fort or dun built upon a small island which is connected to the shore by a stone causeway *(colour plate 1)*. While the majority of the structure has collapsed a coherent stone face could be followed around part of the circumference. The water clarity in the loch was very low and it was not possible to do more than note the major features of the structure. One of the most interesting aspects of this site was a submerged stone mound nearby in the loch. If the island dun is, as would be expected, about 2,000 years old from the Iron Age, it seems likely that the submerged mound must be older. It is possible that the submerged site was robbed to build the island dun but it is not clear what sort of site it was before robbing.

15 Dun Bharabhat island dun, Great Bernera, Isle of Lewis. *N. Dixon*

Bragar Broch, Loch an Duna, Bragar (NB 462597)

This site, while similar in many ways to that in Loch an Duin, was better preserved and not only could the walls be detected around much of the circumference but the entrance with its large lintel stone was obvious. There are a number of structures in the water around the site and walls are easily recognised in the shallows. Further out into the loch, there is also an almost completely submerged stone mound *(6)* except for a few stones projecting above the water that may be a later addition for marking the site. The same speculations as to date and relationship apply as at Loch an Duin.

Loch Bharabhat, Great Bernera (NB 156356)

Dun Bharabhat, an island dun in Loch Bharabhat on the island of Great Bernera, is the best preserved of all the island duns and is a scheduled ancient monument. It still stands high above the water and even the intra-mural galleries, so typical of brochs, are evident from the shore *(15)*. It is hard to imagine what sort of threat motivated the builders to carry the thousands of stones out to an island to build the fort but it is certainly a statement of prestige and power. Undoubtedly there will be well-preserved evidence of the people and their way of life preserved in the cold, dark waters of the surrounding loch.

Loch Bharabhat, Cnip (NB 099353)

There are a number of Loch Bharabhats in the Hebrides. Loch Bharabhat, near the

16 Excavation of island dun in Loch Bharabhat, Cnip, showing wall of drowned structure.
N. Dixon

village of Cnip in the west of Lewis, contains an island dun with a stone causeway leading to the shore. It is included in the RCAHMS (1928 no. 72) where it states that the site was substantially reduced in 1911 to build sheep pens nearby. The walls were still obvious around part of the circumference during the 1985 survey. In the summer of 1985, the first joint land and underwater excavation in the country was begun on this site with fascinating results *(colour plate 3)* (Dixon and Harding 2000).

The aim of the underwater programme here was to locate midden material and other remains associated with the occupation of the dun in the hope of explaining more about the food, clothing and general way of life of the dun-dwellers *(colour plate 4)*. The project exceeded expectations, however, with the discovery of a sub-circular structure submerged in the shallows beside the island *(16)*. Amazingly, if the first 1m-wide trench opened in 1985 had been located just half-a-metre to the north the submerged building may never have been discovered. The building was filled with superimposed compacted floors of peat, straw, and heather from which a wide range of artefacts was recovered. Other floor layers consisted of packing stones, cobbles and white beach sand which were laid to try and stem the water as the structure sank into the loch-bed silts. The floor layers extended to a depth of about 2m underwater at the level of the base of the structure and excavations eventually went almost 3m down into pre-structure levels. Radiocarbon dates indicate that the drowned building is contemporary with the primary occupation of the dun and that it sank before the dun was finally abandoned.

The structure had been built as an ancillary building to the dun and the intact floor layers enclosed within the walls produced clear evidence that it had played a role as a workshop and a byre at different times. Finds of bone and antler tools attested to the workshop phase and layers of animal dung pointed to the use as a byre and many other well-preserved organic finds illustrated the life of the dun-dwellers.

Unfortunately, the builders did not choose the foundation of this part of the site well as it seems to have almost immediately started to sink into the soft loch sediments which could not support the weight. As the wall subsided more stones were added to heighten the wall but, of course, the increased weight added to the problem and caused more subsidence. The floor was clearly getting wet so at different times layers of stones, sand, pebbles, peat and heather were put down to build it up and keep it dry. Eventually, the effort was too great and the building was rebuilt closer to the main dun which was founded on bedrock.

These excavations vividly demonstrate the richness of submerged remains around and in these sites on the Isle of Lewis and it is clear that further underwater excavations in other island duns will add an immense amount of information not available from land sites.

SUMMARY AND CONCLUSIONS

Island duns, small islands with the remains of stone-built duns or brochs, from the last two centuries BC and the first two centuries AD, abound in the Outer Hebrides but the survey indicated that there are other stone mounds, often totally submerged, that may well pre-date them. In some cases the island duns and stone mounds are close together and it has been suggested that the mounds may have been robbed to construct the island duns. It is also possible that these stone mounds are the equivalent of the typical crannog type of site found on the mainland. If so, they would have to be built in a very different manner to the island duns which are almost wholly stone as would be expected in a relatively treeless landscape like the Outer Isles.

CRANNOGS IN THE HIGHLANDS

Loch Tollaidh, Gairloch
In 1992, the Gairloch Heritage Museum requested us to survey Loch Tollaidh and an island with the remains of a small building on it *(17)*. They wanted to determine if the extensive mound of boulders underlying the small island was artificial or natural and to locate occupational evidence relating to the MacBeaths, McLeods, and/or MacKenzies who had inhabited the site in

17 Eilean Tollaidh, Gairloch. *N. Dixon*

the past. Local histories and Murray and Pullar's *Bathymetrical Survey of the Freshwater Lochs of Scotland* gave some background to the loch and the features that might exist in it.

Eilean Loch Tollaidh, Background
According to local history (Dixon 1886), the island was a stronghold inhabited during the thirteenth century by the MacBeaths, originally from Assynt, and others. Dixon refers to the 'castle on the island' but whether this is his own interpretation of the sort of dwelling place that existed or whether he is referring to earlier manuscripts is not stated. The MacBeaths were involved in numerous conflicts with other clans of the area and were eventually ejected from their lands by the McLeods sometime in the early fifteenth century. Presumably at this time they left the island in Loch Tollaidh which was later occupied in 1480 by Allan McLeod, the laird of Gairloch, with his wife and two sons.

Allan McLeod and his sons were murdered by other members of the McLeod clan and as a result, Gairloch was granted by royal charter in 1494 to Hector Roy Mackenzie who had been commissioned in around 1480 to destroy the members of the McLeod clan who had perpetrated the deed. It was around the end of the sixteenth century before the McLeods were finally ousted from the area which came, from then on, under the control of the MacKenzies.

It is not clear at what time the island in Loch Tollaidh was finally abandoned as a stronghold but in 1608, under orders from King James, the Privy Council had the crannogs of the Western Isles torn down as they offered too much protection for the feuding highlanders. The castle, or other structure, in Loch Tollaidh may have been destroyed at this time.

It might be thought that with such a long and recorded history the island would have substantial remains preserved on and around it. In most cases, crannogs are obviously artificial structures with some evidence of occupation such as fragments of pot, charcoal, bone, cut wood, burnt peat and in some cases structural timbers or the outline of stone buildings. The island in Loch Tollaidh turned out to be an exception.

Methodology and Observations
An initial two-day snorkel survey early in 1992, showed what seemed to be a large submerged platform standing clear of deeper loch-bed silts by 1-3m, separated from the shore by a 2m-wide gap at the end of a wide causeway. The edge of the platform appeared to be lined with large stones and the relatively flat, even top looked as if it had been deliberately levelled for habitation. On top of this platform near the middle was a sub-circular raised mound with remains of a small building covered with undergrowth and trees.

According to Murray and Pullar, the remains of a mill could be seen at the outlet of the loch when they were there in 1902. Even then it was 'fast disappearing' and there is little evidence to be seen now. It seemed possible that the platform could be underwater because these foundations were still keeping the water level artificially high.

Submerged platform
The platform is a large and firm flat area, resembling a submerged land surface, in approximately 30cm of water sloping down around the edges to deeper water on the offshore side. Large boulders and patches of what appeared to be bedrock were also noted. Near the trees and up-standing structure on the small island, compact coarse reddish silts overlay what appeared to be white marl-like clay.

The observations from the preliminary survey, the flat, even surface and the large edging stones suggested that the site was at least a heavily modified natural feature if not totally artificial. However, accurate angles and the existence of curvilinear arrangements underwater in low visibility are difficult to observe and define. A more substantial survey later in the year clarified the earlier observations. There was no evidence underwater of obvious walls, timbers or other man-made structural details. There was also no visible evidence of occupation debris that would be expected from a dwelling that had been inhabited for a substantial period of time. After surveying the site with the total station it became apparent that the submerged platform was much less regular than it had appeared from the earlier snorkel and low-visibility diving observations.

Underwater Test Trench

It is more than a little surprising that not one piece of pottery, bone or charcoal was discovered lying on the surface of the submerged platform. However, it was thought that exposed remains may have been washed away or destroyed by mechanical or chemical erosion so a test pit was excavated, to a depth of about 1m, near the edge of the island in the area thought most likely to have been utilised by the inhabitants. There were no remains of materials that might be expected from an area of habitation. The stratified layers observed in the trench section were clearly naturally deposited with no evidence of anthropogenic deposition. It became obvious that the platform was in fact a natural feature and there was no evidence at all of artificial build-up.

The Island

The island, with trees and bushes standing proud of the water appeared to be a circular man-made structure, constructed of regular-sized stones, with a depression in the centre. Habitation on the site is only evident from the remains of a small building on the island. Since the foundations of buildings are often

18 Underwater examination of building foundations on Eilean Tollaidh. B.L. Andrian

sited in a bedding trench, it is reasonable to assume that if the submerged platform was once above water the foundations of the building would now be substantially submerged and dug into the top of the platform. Accordingly, the north face of the building was cleared down to and below water level to expose the lowest courses *(18)*. Two courses of stone were below water level and the bottom one sat on top of the platform and was not cut into the base material. The building could easily have been constructed with the water at its present level and there is therefore no need to assume a lower level at the time of construction.

The 'castle'

The remains above water on the island were of a small building assumed to be the 'castle' referred to in the past. A small sondage was cut across one wall and the outside face was cleared for part of its length uncovering the remnants of a coarse, rubble-built structure. A small animal bone and a mussel shell, both from the later overburden, were the only objects found during the investigation.

CONCLUSIONS

The survey showed that the submerged features are natural and that the visible remains above water are the extent of the habitation on the island relating to the references of past occupation. It is extremely surprising that not one piece of pottery, bone, charcoal or other hearth material was discovered on the extensive, submerged platform and the assumption must be that the material existence of the site's inhabitants was extremely poor, or deliberately removed. This is supported by the coarseness of the building technique employed. Given the substantial oral and written record of the site it seems that the inhabitants played an important part in the traditions of the region but did not leave a large impact on the environment or the occupation site.

The survey of Loch Tollaidh was disappointing for the team but more so for the Gairloch Heritage Museum who had hoped to add an important new dimension to their already impressive displays explaining the past in this beautiful area. To the members of the STUA it showed that not all islands will produce the masses of habitation debris that we have come to expect from water based sites.

LOCHINDORB

Introduction

Lochindorb lies on the border of Elginshire and Nairnshire, in the basin of the River Findhorn into which it drains via the Dorback Burn. The loch is just over two miles long, ⅔ mile wide at the north end and ⅓ mile wide at the south end and covers an area of 219 hectares. The maximum depth of the loch is around 17m, the mean is 4m and about half of the area of the loch is less than 4m deep. The surrounding area is typical of Highland Scotland with few trees and a blanket of heather and bracken. There is some cultivated land near the edge of the loch and tradition refers to significant woodlands around the loch in the past. At present, a peat bog containing many tree stumps is being eroded into the south end of the loch.

The castle in the loch, associated with the Comyn family, is believed to have been constructed in the thirteenth century. King Edward I is attributed with making impressive fortifications there in 1303 but its most notable inhabitant was Alexander Stewart, the 'Wolf of Badenoch', who occupied the castle until the early fifteenth century. It was destroyed in 1458 and is now a substantial ruin and a scheduled ancient monument *(colour plate 5)*.

In 1993, we were asked to carry out a survey in the loch, on behalf of a local group of interested divers known as the Lochindorb Heritage Team. The group wanted to establish whether the castle sits on an earlier artificial island and whether other submerged features relate to the castle or to earlier occupation. We specifically examined the find spot of a large ceramic jar that had been raised from the loch bed the year before to take advantage of the depression remaining in the loch-bed silts to observe possible earlier material. Over the years a number of objects, including the jar, have been raised from the loch and some are now in Inverness Museum.

Loch Survey

Lochindorb was surveyed by Murray and Pullar at the beginning of the twentieth century (Murray and Pullar 1905). Past experience has shown that their surveys are usually accurate so it was with surprise that a number of anomalies, in the form of very shallow areas, were discovered in the loch. In two cases where a depth of more than 7m had been noted the actual depth was found to be less than 1m. There is no evidence that the loch bottom has changed since the time of their survey and the conclusion is that the survey was not detailed enough to pick up these features.

Submerged forest

At the south end of the loch the remains of ancient woodlands were seen in the face of an eroding peat bank. Substantial stumps of trees, identified as Scots Pine, can be seen projecting from the peat face above water level and underwater scattered on the loch bed for more than 100m from the shore *(colour plate 6)*. A sample from one of the timbers produced a radiocarbon date of 6530±60 BP (calibrated to 5611-5330 BC) from the Neolithic period.

Presumably the forest grew in a warmer period and was destroyed and buried by peat growth when the weather deteriorated.

Archaeological survey of main island

The castle island in Lochindorb measured approximately 100m across at its widest point. The ruins of the Medieval castle take up most of the area of the island above water but observations underwater suggest that the mound may have been artificially constructed prior to the building of the castle.

On the west side the underwater profile is a gentle slope which gradually merges with the loch bed. Many of the stones which make up the mound at this point appear to have been artificially deposited but the wide range in size and type could also point to natural, geological origins. Underwater survey on the south and east sides revealed a composition which is much more artificial in appearance. The angle of slope is steeper and the more homogeneous size of stones is similar to sites elsewhere which are accepted as being of artificial construction.

The submerged area on the north side of the island has clearly man-made features, in the shape of fallen walls. Away from the obvious remains of the castle the loch bed slopes gently to the north where layers of what appear to be natural clay can be seen with large cracks running through them. It is not clear how these breaks were formed but in the past, lochs were often dredged for a limey clay, known as marl, which was put on the fields as manure for agricultural improvement.

Fallen walls

One of the most interesting discoveries was in the shallows off the north side of the island where there are a number of supposedly fallen walls. These were planned and drawn as part of the survey record. It has been suggested that these walls are the remains of one of the castle curtain walls pulled down during the destruction of 1458. However, while some of the alignments appear to be in a collapsed and sloping state others are vertical. It seems unlikely that the top of a wall, some 10m high, would land upright in a coherent manner, still substantially intact, on the loch bed if it were pulled down. The plans produced during the survey also show the walls in a relatively restricted area immediately to the east of the present landing place. Since mounds of stones on shore representing the fallen wall extend almost to the north-east corner of the island it may be queried as to why the fallen remains underwater do not extend all the way to the corner.

The possibility cannot be ignored that the remains represent another feature, such as a landing stage or small harbour, or an earlier feature such as the robbed outer walls of a pre-castle structure. This can only be established with further examination and the excavation of one or more of the submerged walls.

Early references to submerged timber structures
Near the submerged walls was a large oak beam projecting from the loch bed and possibly associated with them. Early observers referred to oak beams beneath the water:

> Great rafts or planks of oak, by the beating of the waters against the old walls, occasionally make their appearance, which confirms an opinion entertained of this place, that it had been a national business, originally built upon an artificial island. (Old Statistical Account, *vol. viii, p 259*)

It is possible that the beam observed during the survey is one of these and represents the remains of an earlier crannog.

Other reports spoke of a possible causeway leading to the shore which could date from the period of the castle or from the time of an earlier structure. Survey of the loch bottom between the island and the shore brought to light a number of gravel ridges but closer examination suggested that they were natural features with no evidence of artificial construction.

Pot-hole
In 1992 a large storage jar was discovered by a local diver and lifted from the shallows off the north-east corner of the island. In lifting the pot the bottom sediments were disturbed and a small trench enclosing this area was excavated to establish whether there were any other associated finds and whether stratigraphy was recognisable within the upper loch bed sediments. Bearing in mind that the island above water is a scheduled ancient monument and that the present work was intended to be a non-disturbance survey the trench was kept as small as possible. Eventually an area less than 0.25m square was excavated below the level of the uppermost silts.

The upper layers consisted of very modern fine silt overlying more compacted silts. The compact layer of silt contained cut wood, pot-handle fragments and the complete pot that had been raised earlier, and had ultimately initiated the survey. The pot dated these layers to the fifteenth century and the occupation of the castle. The layer immediately below the layer with the pot contained cut wood, charcoal, burnt peat and other organic debris and must relate either to an earlier phase of castle occupation or to occupation of the island prior to the construction of the castle.

Stone shot
During the search for the causeway, five stone balls, believed to be granite, were discovered measuring from 24-28cm in diameter *(19)*. They all lay about 25-30m from the island, between it and the shore, and it is believed that they were

19 Trebuchet shot on lochbed near Lochindorb Castle. *B.L. Andrian*

stone shot fired from a trebuchet. Documentary sources recorded that a siege engine was used by Sir Andrew Murray when he besieged the castle in 1335 but that it was not powerful enough to reach the castle. It is exciting and unusual to find such shot in situ and vividly demonstrates the use of powerful siege engines at this time.

A certain amount of data is already available about the performance of the trebuchet as a full-scale reconstruction was made in Denmark in 1989 (Hansen 1990). The machine weighed 12 tons and could throw a stone ball, weighing 15kg (33lb), a distance of 180m. A counterweight of 2,000kg (4,409lb) was used to achieve this result but the machine was designed to take up to 4,000kg (8,818lb) so greater distance was possible.

At Lochindorb, the distance from the shore to the castle wall is 265m and 310m to the centre of the courtyard. It would appear that the first firing efforts during the siege fell short and presumably more weight was added to give greater range.

Boat

In the shallow water on the east side of the island a few planks and a knee from a small boat were observed. The remains were not deeply embedded in the loch bed and were possibly associated with the same layer of loch-bed silt that contained the pot. Since the boat remains were close to the pot-find and the discovery of four other fragments of pot handle, it is possible that there is a relationship between them. One explanation is that pots were being transported in the boat when it sank. Some pots may have been recovered leaving remains of four handles and possibly one complete pot behind. The pots may have been empty since the complete example raised in 1992 was found without a stopper.

SUMMARY AND CONCLUSIONS

The 1993 preliminary survey was successful in its main aims as it provided some understanding of the loch, the island and the sediments of the loch. While no conclusive evidence of pre-castle occupation was found, the results of the small-scale sondage indicate the presence of rich layers of stratified organic material. Conditions in the loch are such that underwater survey and excavation could be carried out to the highest archaeological standards.

The Lochindorb Heritage Team, although untrained in archaeology, is eager to take professional advice and to acquire the necessary skills with which to further the project.

CRANNOGS IN CENTRAL SCOTLAND

There are many crannogs recorded in Central Scotland and Lochend Loch; Coatbridge excavated in the 1930s (see above) is typical. A brief survey identified two crannogs in Linlithgow Loch but no detailed work has been done to examine and plan them in detail. Possibly the best-known loch in the world is Loch Lomond and survey work has gone on there on two occasions with the most complete survey in 1997.

Loch Lomond Survey

In 1988, the STUA carried out a brief survey at the south end of Loch Lomond concentrating on one area in particular, Cameron Bay, which was examined in some depth. A submerged mound, marked by a small, stone lighthouse, was surveyed with a view to future excavation. A small sondage cut into the top of the mound brought to light a number of small timbers that were clearly aligned to each other as part of early structure on the site. Radiocarbon dates from the timbers came out at 210±80 BC and 40±50 BC (GU-2439 and GU-2440). What was not obvious at that time was the existence of another lower circular mound close by which is best seen on aerial photographs *(20)*.

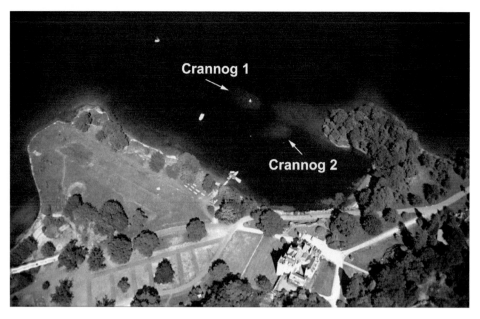

20 Locations of two crannogs in Cameron Bay, Loch Lomond. *D.W. Harding*

In 1997, the STUA was asked to survey Loch Lomond for FIRAT Archaeological Services who were carrying out a full-scale survey on behalf of the Friends of Loch Lomond. The survey started with a list of 28 target sites which had been collected from local knowledge, historical references and earlier surveys. It is always particularly exciting to examine well-known lochs and Loch Lomond is known throughout the world as one of Scotland's most beautiful attractions.

Loch Lomond is an odd loch. It is a combination of a typical long, narrow, deep Highland type of loch in the north and a typical lowland loch in the south. This is because the Highland Boundary Fault Line runs through the middle of the loch and can be seen in a line of large islands across the loch.

From the 28 targets, the remains of 10 crannogs were discovered in the loch and all of them in the south end. Some of the sites are stony mounds with some exciting features and even more intriguing locations and depths within the loch which has been raised since the outflow was regulated. Ten crannogs in a loch the size of Loch Lomond may not seem a large number compared to Loch Tay and Loch Awe, however, there are 34 natural islands in the loch and clear evidence that many of these were also inhabited.

Swan Island
One of the reasons for carrying out the survey was to see whether there were any dangers to the crannogs in the loch. At Swan Island, which makes an attractive

addition to the scenery of the area, this was seen to be the case. Boats have been moored on and beside the island for a very long time *(colour plate 7)* and it is clear that the loch has been seen as a useful dumping ground for all sorts of material. Much of this is old metal which is now rusting down into the water and the site, potentially damaging the fragile remains and adversely affecting the chances of obtaining useful radiocarbon dates in the future.

Mechanical damage is also obvious from the chains and mooring lines attached to the island. They are being dragged back and forth in the currents and in a number of places are eroding the surface of the island and exposing earlier material which is, of course, immediately destroyed.

CRANNOGS IN SOUTH-WEST SCOTLAND

In 1989, the STUA carried out a survey in the south-west of Scotland on behalf of what used to be the Nature Conservancy Council of Scotland (now Scottish Natural Heritage) and Historic Scotland. The main aim of the survey was to establish whether lochs were being affected by nutrient inflows from agriculture and forestry causing damage to the delicate organic remains on the crannogs in the area. This is the homeland of some of Robert Munro's best work and there are many crannogs in the lochs.

The STUA selected a number of lochs for examination, some deliberately because they had been recorded in the past and it would be interesting to see if the reports from as much as 100 years ago could be verified. Two of the most interesting lochs investigated were Milton Loch, where a crannog had been excavated in 1950, and Loch Arthur, where the longest logboat in Scotland was discovered in the nineteenth century. A number of examples point to the richness of this area and sites in it and to the damage that is being caused by nutrients running into the water from adjacent agricultural land (Dixon 1989b).

Milton Loch

Milton Loch Crannog was first excavated by Mrs C.M. Piggott in 1950. Her work was considered the best on crannogs for many years (see above). Her excavations exposed hundreds of well-preserved timbers on and around the site and she was able to reconstruct the site as it might have been when it was occupied with some degree of confidence. Our survey in 1989 showed that the timbers she planned and excavated and particularly the many piles surrounding the site were still very obviously sticking up from the loch-bed silts. Samples were taken for dating and a radiocarbon date of 130±50 BC (GU-2648) was obtained which falls a little later than the dates of 490±100 BC (K-2027) and one taken a little later which was 400±100 BC (K-1394) discussed above.

We also noted another crannog in the loch that had been recorded by Piggott but which had not been examined. Snorkelling around the site showed that it too was surrounded by many upright piles and one of these gave a date of 110±50 BC (GU-2647). Unexpectedly, a third island in the middle of the loch, which had not been recorded in Piggott's original report, was found with upright piles in the loch bed around it and two radiocarbon dates came out at 480±50 AD (GU-2645) and 480±70 AD (GU-2646) indicating that the loch was used by crannog-dwellers for almost 1,000 years. It is perhaps not surprising that in this area, Munro's centre of research in the nineteenth century, even a small loch has the remains of three sites with visible timbers from as early as the Iron Age, 2,500 years ago.

Loch Arthur

This loch is notable as being the find spot for the longest logboat in Scotland which was discovered here in the nineteenth century. The front end of the boat can now be seen in the basement of the new National Museum of Scotland in Edinburgh. The most surprising aspect of the find is that this 15m long vessel was in such a small loch where it could hardly have been used to full effect as a means of transport. Small steps carved into the inner bows of the boat possibly suggest a ritualistic function.

The crannog in the loch is a large, substantial island with trees growing on top. Vertical and horizontal timbers were noted around the site and two samples gave radiocarbon dates of 290±60 BC and 310±50 BC (GU-2644, GU-2643) The water was full of insects and insect larvae cases which may have multiplied owing to the raised nutrients and eutrophication of the water.

These two examples from the south-west of Scotland are only two of many and in this rich farming area it is likely that many others are also being adversely affected by agricultural run-off. Survey of the crannogs in the area is still going on.

CRANNOGS IN PERTHSHIRE

The STUA is based at Loch Tay in Perthshire and research work has gone on in the loch for 25 years so it is not surprising that this area has had more survey in recent years than most others. A number of lochs have been examined including very small examples like Loch Clunie and the very large Loch Tay and all have produced exciting and often surprising results.

Loch of Clunie

The Loch of Clunie is one of a group of small lochs in the Tay drainage basin. It is situated between the Loch of Craiglush and the Loch of the Lowes in the west and the Loch of Drumellie in the east, lying along the Lunan Burn which drains into the River Isla which in turn joins the River Tay. The area is rich in archaeological sites from all dates, many of them from the prehistoric period. A number of islands in the lochs of the area may be the remains of crannogs and there may well be other submerged features relating to early periods.

The Loch
The Loch of Clunie is an attractive small loch in wooded farmland in east Perthshire. It was surveyed in 1903 by Murray and Pullar for their *Bathymetrical Survey of the Freshwater Lochs of Scotland*. The chart shows the positions of an island *(9)*, on which Clunie Castle stands, a submerged mound reputedly a crannog, and their relationship with the natural features of the loch bed. The island which supports the castle '... seems to be artificial ...' and the submerged mound of stones off the north shore was '... said to have been put down to indicate a sandbank' (Murray and Pullar 1910, 103-04).

The island with the castle is referred to in a number of documents. When he was Secretary of the Society of Antiquaries of Scotland in 1866, John Stuart recorded in the first systematic survey of crannogs, 'Loch of Cluny, Perthshire. Enlarged and fortified by an artificial barrier of stones' (Stuart 1866, 178). Robert Munro, in his list of sites in *Ancient Scottish Lake Dwellings*, was equally terse with the entry, 'A small island, mostly artificial, with ruins of an old castle' (Munro 1882, 246). He stated his source as the *Old Statistical Account of Scotland* (OSA), vol. ix, p 231.

The same OSA reference was brought to the attention of the Rev. F.O. Blundell and incorporated in a paper to the Society of Antiquaries relating to artificial islands in the Highlands (Blundell 1912, 261). The OSA reporter, Rev. W. MacRitchie, referred to papers from around AD 1500 which mentioned 'the island of the Loch of Clunie'. He also mentioned local traditions of the island once being joined to the shore on the south-east side but points out that the water on that side is deep and that the closest point to the island is on the west shore making that the most likely line of any causeway that might have existed.

MacRitchie was of the opinion that the island was artificial, as he stated:

> ... that this island has been formed principally by human art seems demonstrable from this, that the ground of which it is composed is evidently factitious; and in lately digging to the depth of 7 feet, near the centre of the island, nothing like a natural stratum of earth appeared. The foundation of the castle wall is several feet below the surface of the water, and in all probability rests on piles of oak. (*Blundell 1912, 263*)

The castle was built as a retreat by Bishop Brown of Dunkeld between 1485 and 1514 and included the religious structure of St Catherine's Chapel which no longer exists. The site was substantially modified and restored around the end of the eighteenth century and was inhabited until very recently. When the last occupants left, the castle was damaged by fire and it is now an abandoned, roofless ruin although there are still interesting features in the lower rooms that were not damaged by the fire. The site is now a scheduled monument as are the other features in the loch and on the nearby shore.

Only Murray and Pullar refer to the mound of stones off the north shore of the loch and they did not refer to it other than as a marker of shallow water. On their chart of the loch they marked the site of the mound with a circle of dots with one in the middle and placed it between the 3m and 7.5m submarine contours. In other cases where they recognised stone mounds as crannogs they marked them as such on their charts.

The Ordnance Survey on their 1:25,000 series maps show the position of the mound and mark it as a crannog (OS Sheet NO 04/14, Pathfinder 324, Series 1:25,000).

Survey by the STUA

A survey of remains in the Loch of Clunie was carried out for the Royal Commission on the Ancient and Historical Monuments of Scotland to establish more accurately the form of the island and the mound of stones. A deadline of March 1991 for the report meant that the work had to be carried out in the first two months of the year, a time not best suited to underwater examination as visibility is not normally good and the water is extremely cold, leading to reduced dive times. The first reconnaissance trip showed that it was not possible to carry out any underwater work as thick ice still covered the submerged mound and surrounded the castle island making access difficult and dangerous. The survey was eventually carried out when the loch was substantially, though not completely, free of ice.

Crannog (NO114444)

The submerged mound was located using an echo sounder and visual search. It is slightly oval and about 8m in diameter and was 0.6m under water at its highest point. It has been constructed on the edge of a natural ridge which slopes down steeply into deeper water. In some places it was clear to see where the stones of the mound gave way to the surrounding loch bed but in others the transition was obscured by soft silt. The loch bed around the mound was examined and, like the mound, was found to be covered with yellow/brown soft silt which immediately clouded the water when disturbed.

Stones project up through the silt and a large timber, embedded in stones and silt, was noted close to the north-west side of the mound. The timber is approximately 3.0m long and 0.6m wide with a shallow groove running along part of its length. One end was exposed and had been cut across, but visibility was too poor to observe any detail. It is likely that this is the remains of a structural timber which has survived because it is oak, and therefore very hard. It is possible that this timber was part of a structure once built on the loch bed, but without disturbance of the bottom this could not be ascertained.

The basic outline of the possible crannog was planned with tapes, compass and the echo sounder and a contour survey of the mound and its environs was completed, drawn from more than 500 soundings.

While there is little evidence to show whether the mound of stones was built as a beacon to warn of shallow water or as a settlement site, our experience in examining similar sites elsewhere suggests that the Loch of Clunie mound and associated shallows are the remains of an early artificial structure. The mound would represent a very small site with a diameter of only 8m, but the stones themselves need not represent the past extent of a crannog especially if the whole of the shallow area is part of the same structure. This would produce an elongated site measuring about 25m by 13m making it similar to a number of crannogs elsewhere. The overall form of the features with a stone mound overlying another differently shaped raised area is not unusual and examples may be seen in other lochs.

Castle Island (NO113440)

Bearing in mind the comments by MacRitchie (see above) regarding the artificiality of the island, a cursory examination was made of the surface. No bedrock was seen to suggest a natural foundation but there were no other indications of artificial construction. However, examination of the perimeter of the island and the shallow water around it showed the boulder make-up typical of crannogs in many parts of the country.

It was not practicable to examine large parts of the perimeter as there are many fallen trees and branches in the shallow water near the shore. Diving among these in low visibility is dangerous as it is possible to become trapped. Nevertheless, in the areas that were exposed, the low wall that surrounds part of the island were seen to sit on top of underlying boulders.

The boulders slope down under water from the edge of the island until they merge with, and become covered by, the silt of the loch bed. It is not clear without probing substantial areas whether there is an obvious edge to the area of boulders but observations made elsewhere would suggest that they are not naturally deposited. One of the most comparable sites is Priory Island in Loch Tay (Dixon 1982, 20) which is bigger than Loch Clunie Castle Island but shows the same circular plan, the same boulder construction and still supports a substantial ruin that was inhabited until the eighteenth century. Both sites have early references to their occupation and it is possible that they were originally built as early as the prehistoric era.

The castle island is also likely to be of a wholly artificial construction. Its position at the edge of the drop-off into deeper water and the make-up of evenly-sized stones is similar to many artificial islands throughout the country and these features are not likely to be the result of natural deposition.

The most obvious route for a causeway from the island to the shore would be south and then west skirting the deeper depression. However, a number of profiles taken across this line with the echo sounder showed no indication of such a causeway. The depth, around 1.8-2.4m, would have necessitated a raised walkway rather than a causeway built up from the bed of the loch and the evidence for such a walkway may be hidden beneath the silts of the loch bed.

SUMMARY AND CONCLUSIONS

The survey carried out in the Loch of Clunie covered the area of the supposed crannog off the north shore, the environs of the island on which Clunie Castle is situated and the area off the west shore and the motte. Many sonar runs were also made over the rest of the loch using the hydrograph and these support the overall accuracy of Murray and Pullar's chart indicating a maximum depth of 23m. The results of the survey are inconclusive, as is often the case with initial non-disturbance surveys, but they are useful in indicating the possible artificiality of the structures in the loch. They also give a base from which to consider further work which would include sondages to acquire samples for environmental analysis and radiocarbon dating. In the case of Loch Clunie this would require the consent of Historic Scotland as the sites are scheduled ancient monuments.

LOCH TAY SURVEY

Loch Tay Background

Loch Tay is one of the most beautiful and scenic areas of Scotland. It is relatively untouched by tourism, given its proximity to the main urban centres of Scotland – one-and-a-half hours to Glasgow and two hours to Edinburgh. But with the rise in leisure time over the last 20 years, this is changing.

In the nineteenth century Loch Tay was seen as a perfectly viable day-trip venue. The train to Killin could be boarded in Edinburgh, at Killin the steamship picked up the passengers and took them to Kenmore, or other places along the loch. Later, the train safely delivered the passengers back to Edinburgh. Of course, the end of the steamships and the railways in the southern Highlands put an end to these trips.

Probably the most famous visitor to the area was Queen Victoria who came on her honeymoon in 1842. She was highly impressed by the people and the place. Hardly surprising given the immense efforts the then Marquis of Breadalbane went to entertain her. But the weather seems to have cooperated at the time as well.

The islands in the loch add to the beauty and interest of the scenery and they have always been important for security. It is only 300 years since Priory Island, near Kenmore, was abandoned and it was the last inhabited artificial island of many in a tradition that began more than 2,500 years ago. The crannogs of Loch Tay are the remnants of the history of the area. They are being excavated now with the aid of the most modern techniques of underwater archaeology which are bringing to light astonishing and exciting material preserved by the dark and peaty waters of the loch. The past can be immensely relevant to the present and to the development of the future.

Location of crannogs

The shape of the loch and its submerged features are made clear by the hydrographic charts produced by Murray and Pullar when they published their *Bathymetrical Survey of the Freshwater Lochs of Scotland* at the beginning of this century. They showed the deepest part of the loch to be 169m but modern sailors have recorded over 183m.

The slopes of the loch edge underwater can be very steep. However, the ends of the loch are shallower and it is here that the majority of the crannogs are located. Both ends have been affected by silt deposition which has created broad shallow areas. At the Killin end of the loch the effects of silting mean that some of the crannogs appear much smaller than they really are and in the case of Eilean Puttychan it is now a peninsula joined to the shore, just off Finlarig Castle, surrounded by very shallow water.

Numerous burns run into Loch Tay and they have been important in creating alluvial fans of sediments in the loch, shallow enough to build crannogs upon. These are best seen at Ardeonaig and Dall where there are four crannogs very close to each other. Also, at Fearnan where there are two crannogs. Not much further out from these sites the loch bottom drops off very steeply showing that the crannog-builders of the past were well aware of the features and profile of the loch bed.

Archaeology

Surprisingly there are few remains of early habitation of prehistoric times around the shores of the valley of Loch Tay. Contrasting with the mass of remains of

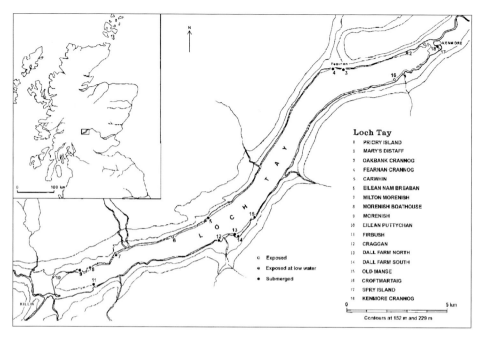

21 Distribution of crannogs in Loch Tay.

houses and settlements from the last 200 years whose inhabitants were evicted in the clearances.

There is evidence of earlier populations but so far the remains of their houses and settlements have not yet been discovered. For instance, the so-called axe factory near Killin indicates the presence of Neolithic settlement about 5,000 years ago. The number of Bronze Age cup- and ring-marked rocks on the slopes around the loch show occupation 3,000-4,000 years ago. But the typical hillforts, hut platforms and other settlement types of Iron Age Scotland are not found. Drummond Hill, above Kenmore, is the only site according to the distribution maps. It is evident that the part normally played by those settlement types was, in some cases, taken over by the crannogs found in the loch.

The crannogs of Loch Tay

In Loch Tay there are the remains of artificial island dwellings which were inhabited by the people who lived in this area over the last 2,600 years. A survey of the loch carried out in 1979 brought to light the definite remains of 18 sites *(21)*. They are in a superb state of preservation because they are submerged in the cold peaty waters of the loch. One of these sites, Oakbank Crannog, has set a precedent as the first in Britain to be excavated underwater.

Even 300 years ago it was known that the loch contained the remains of a number of artificial islands. The evidence was well-outlined by Gillies in his excellent history of the area, *In Famed Breadalbane* first published in 1938 and recently republished. The early tradition spoke of 24 sites and Gillies gave approximate positions for 13.

Five of the sites are islands and are well-known features in the landscape.

Priory Island (NN 766454)
Also known as the Isle of Loch Tay and Eilean nam Ban (Island of the Women) this is the largest of the islands in Loch Tay *(colour plate 8)*. When it was first surveyed in 1979 we thought it was probably natural, as it was so big, but closer examination shows that it is almost certainly of artificial construction. The island is first noted in a charter signed at Stirling by Alexander I granting it to the monks of Scone Abbey which he had recently founded. This grant was reputedly as a result of the death of Alexander's consort, Queen Sybilla, who became ill and died on the island on 12 June 1122 and was subsequently buried there. Later, the island was the fortified home of the Campbells of Glenorchy and ruins of a building, probably erected by Duncan the second Earl of Glenorchy after a destructive fire on Palm Sunday 1509, still stand to a substantial height. No evidence is available for the date of construction of the island but a reference to a Ewan MacDougall of the district has the statement by him, 'this island, with 23 more of lesser size was built in the loch at the expense of King Alexander the First of Scotland'. This is not so, as the known islands and underwater mounds in Loch Tay do not have common styles, levels or dates. Three of the sites have been radiocarbon dated to more than 2,000 years ago.

Priory Island is marked on Blaeu's Atlas of 1769 and is probably one of three settlements indicated in the loch on Mercator's map of 1620. The size of the island suggests that it may originally have been the home of the local chief.

Eilean Puttychan (NN 582343)
Also known as Eilean Sputachan (Island of the Little Spout), this peninsula lies around 100m west of Killin Pier, at the westernmost end of the loch. The loch is very shallow here due to extensive silting which has resulted in what was once an island becoming a peninsula *(22)*. The whole mound is in very shallow water with around 1m depth on the east side at the deepest point. In an early document of 1568 Sir Colin Campbell of Glenorchy let lands of Morenish Wester to Patrick Campbell, brother to Duncan Campbell of Glenlyon. The yearly rent was to be 'a sheaf of arrows, if required' and the new tenant had powers to set six small nets around the island and to erect a stable on it. He also had to make his residence on the island or on the land of which it was a part. This is probably the westernmost of the three settlements shown in the loch on Mercator's map of 1620.

22 Eilean Puttychan, post-Medieval crannog near Killin, Loch Tay. M. Brooks

Eilean nam Breaban (NN 641362)

This island is also known as Ellan a Brippan, Ilane Brebane, Isla Brebane and is translated as Island of the Boot Soles. It is near the north shore of the loch and is exposed all year round. It is artificial but an outcrop of natural rock, which can be seen underwater on the west side has provided a solid foundation *(colour plate 9)*. The actual shape of the crannog is substantially different from the structure seen above water. The mound extends to the south-west beneath the surface giving a roughly circular shape to the whole crannog. A charter of 1526 transfers the lands of Carwhin, adjacent to the island, from Haldane of Gleneagles to James Campbell of Lawers. The island is here referred to as Ila Brebane and in another charter of 1546 it is called Ilane Brebane. In Blaeu's Atlas of 1769 it is shown as Ellan a Brippan and in Mercator's map of 1620 this island is the most likely candidate for the central of the three sites marked in Loch Tay. A recent radiocarbon sample dates the island to 430±50 AD (GU12124).

Croftmartaig Island (NN 751437)

Part of this crannog, near the village of Acharn, is exposed all year round although it is almost wholly under water in winter. The area above the surface is roughly circular while underwater the mound extends to the south-west almost the same distance again. The underwater section may be the original structure with the higher area added at a later date. Alternatively, the lower south-west area may have been some form of pier or small harbour for landing and mooring boats.

Spry Island (NN 773452)

Also known as Spar or Spray Island, this site is exposed all year round and stands to a height of around 3m above the average water level in Kenmore Bay at the east end of the loch. Above water it is 40m x 15m, the long axis running east to west. Modifications in shape and size were carried out by the Marquis of Breadalbane for the visit by Queen Victoria in 1842. Remains of a wall can still be seen on the west side dating from these modifications, and mature trees planted then still flourish here. The composition of the island shows it to be artificial but no timbers could be seen which were definitely of the original structure. This is an area of fairly rapid silting so the top of the mound may once have been higher above the loch bed than at present. The island appears on Blaeu's Atlas.

Submerged crannogs

There are thirteen submerged crannogs in the loch. Eight are totally submerged at all times while the other five can just be seen projecting above the surface in summer when the loch level is low. Two submerged sites lie in Fearnan Bay. Oakbank Crannog (NN 726442) has been excavated underwater since 1980 and is the site which the reconstruction at the Scottish Crannog Centre is based on. Radiocarbon dates for the site fall between 400 and 595 BC which is the Early Iron Age in Scotland. Not far away from Oakbank to the west is another crannog (NN 721443), opposite the hotel in Fearnan, with a radiocarbon date of 525 BC indicating that the two dwellings were inhabited at the same time.

Another site (NN 602339) which has been dated lies off Edinburgh University's outdoor centre of Firbush Point near Killin. Structural timbers associated with the site gave a radiocarbon date of 190 BC showing that it was inhabited in the Iron Age but 200-300 years after Oakbank Crannog was abandoned. Examination of this site will add greatly to our understanding of cultural development in the last half of the first millennium BC.

A number of other submerged sites are found in the shallows around the loch. All of them are related to land that would have been good for cultivation in the past. They range in depth from those that just come to the surface when the loch level is low in summer to those that are more than a metre under the surface even in a dry summer. There are three sites in successive bays from Milton Morenish (23) to the west (NN 613353, NN 600347, NN 595346), another off the farm of Tombreck (NN 659371) and another near the Old Manse (NN 682371) just east of Ardeonaig. There is also a broken down mound of material near the old pier on the north side of Kenmore Bay which appears to be the remains of a crannog that was either destroyed by the propeller wash from steamships when the pier was in use, or which was deliberately pulled down as a hazard to steamers coming into the pier and another site, Mary's Distaff (NN 757450), is submerged for most of the year just west of Priory Island.

Two crannogs (NN 672363, NN 674362) off the farm of Dall on the south shore, are particularly important *(24)*. They are very close together but one is substantially deeper and smaller than the other. This suggests that one may have been used and then abandoned when the loch level changed after which time the other was built. The information which can be extracted from these sites will tell us important details about the loch and its environment in the prehistoric past thousands of years ago. The two sites together are more interesting than one by itself and a similar site (NN 664360) off the Craggan Boys' Brigade camp near Ardeonaig, may well add to that story.

It is obvious that the majority of the crannogs in Loch Tay are not open to viewing by casual visitors. Conditions in the loch are often not even good enough for divers or boat users to see the sites which are submerged at all times of the year. Nevertheless, there are many good viewing points for the crannogs that are still islands or, in summer, those that are partly exposed when the loch is low. Even the surroundings of the submerged sites and the lands that were available for the use of the inhabitants are both interesting and enlightening.

Kenmore

Some of the most attractive views of the Loch and some of the most interesting sites can be seen from the beautiful village of Kenmore. From the bridge at Kenmore to the west are the mountains of the Lawers range with Ben Lawers itself in the background. In the loch 500m from the bridge is the dark mass of Priory Island. Between the bridge and the island, the Marquis of Breadalbane used to anchor his steam yacht, the *Carlotta*. The yacht is famous as having sunk in Aberfeldy High Street when a drain gave way as it was being transported to the loch but it now lies in the silts of the loch near the island.

The best view of Kenmore Bay is from the viewpoint in the forest on Drummond Hill *(colour plate 10)*. The crannogs of Priory Island and Spry Island can be seen very clearly and the reconstruction is also obvious on the opposite side of the loch. Croftmartaig Crannog can be seen from the south road as it rises just west of Acharn and further along the road there is a very pleasant long distance view of Eilean Breaban. When the sun is setting in the west this is particularly beautiful. Eilean Puttychan is best seen from the old railway line on the south shore near Finlarig Castle.

1 Iron Age island dun in Loch an Duin, Isle of Lewis. *N. Dixon*

2 The Loch of Kinellan crannog excavated by Fraser in 1917. *N. Dixon*

3 Island dun in Loch Bharabhat, Cnip during excavation. *N. Dixon*

4 Underwater excavation of island dun in Loch Bharabhat, Cnip. *N. Dixon*

5 Lochindorb Castle. Once home of the 'Wolf of Badenoch'. *N. Dixon*

6 Pine stumps eroding from peat bed, Lochindorb. *N. Dixon*

7 Swan Island, Loch Lomond. *STUA*

8 Priory Island, Loch Tay with ruins of last Campbell stronghold. *N. Dixon*

9 Eilean Breaban, Loch Tay. Bedrock can be seen through the water. *M. Brooks*

10 Kenmore Bay, Loch Tay, with Priory Island in the foreground and Spry Island in the background. *N. Dixon*

11 Equipment necessary for underwater archaeological field survey. *B.L. Andrian*

12 Diving operations platform at Oakbank Crannog, Loch Tay. *N. Dixon*

13 Removing small stones from Oakbank Crannog. *N. Dixon*

14 The two-person water dredge for removing spoil and keeping water clear. *B.L. Andrian*

15 Total station survey of Craggan Crannog, Loch Tay. *N. Dixon*

16 Measuring the angle of slope of piles at Oakbank Crannog. *B.L. Andrian*

17 Aerial view of Oakbank Crannog, Loch Tay with Fearnan village in background. *J. Beck*

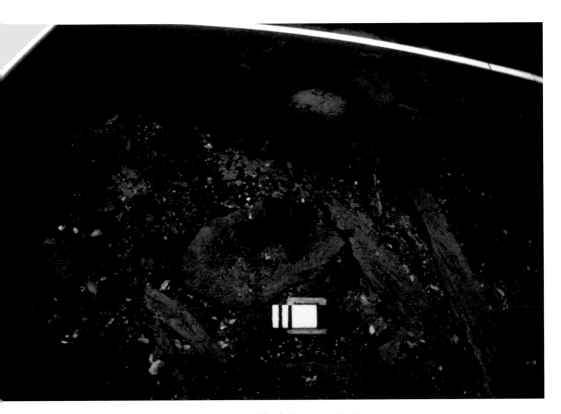

18 Upper stones overlying the organic matrix at Oakbank Crannog. *N. Dixon*

19 Excavating a bundle of hazel withies at Oakbank Crannog. *B.L. Andrian*

20 Excavating a wooden bowl through which a pile was driven in antiquity. *B.L. Andrian*

21 Right Wooden butter dish from Oakbank Crannog. Numbers mark butter sample points. *N. Dixon*

22 Below Wooden whistle made of dogrose from Oakbank Crannog. *N. Dixon*

0   5 cm

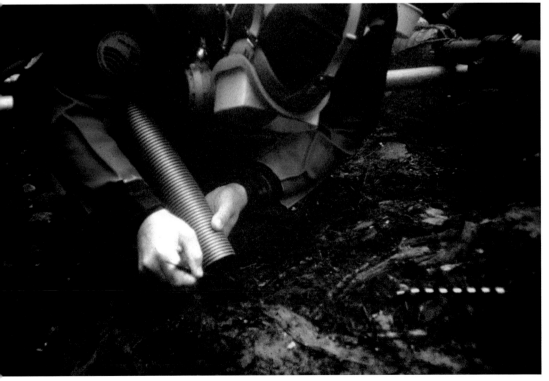

23 Excavating a hazel knot from Oakbank Crannog. *B.L. Andrian*

24 Stone artefacts from Oakbank, including jet and stone beads, spindle whorl a loom weights. *N. Dixon*

25 Artist's impression of a crannog based on Oakbank. *Mason*

26 *Left* Scale model of Oakbank Crannog by David Jones. *N. Dixon*

27 *Opposite* Attempting to drive a small pile as an archaeological experiment. *Andrian*

28 Opposite Driving a large pile at the full-sized crannog reconstruction, Scottish Crannog Centre, Loch Tay. *B.L. Andrian*

29 Above Reconstruction of an Iron Age crannog based on results of excavations at Oakbank Crannog, Loch Tay. *B.L. Andrian*

30 The Scottish Crannog Centre, Reconstruction and Exhibition Centre, Kenmore, Loch Tay. *N. Dixon*

23 Milton Morenish Crannog, Loch Tay. *M. Brooks*

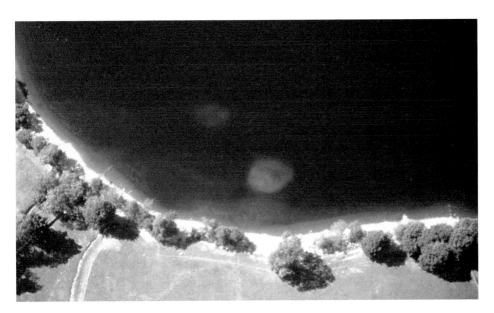

24 Two submerged crannogs in Dall Bay, south shore of Loch Tay. *D.W. Harding*

Of course, most of the sites are completely submerged but the view of the bays in which they lie is very attractive although it takes the eye of imagination to see the area as it would have existed in the prehistoric period.

Loch Tay has been the focus of my work for 25 years and it is still developing. I first surveyed the crannogs in the loch in 1979 and resurveyed them in 2000 with more modern equipment. Satisfyingly the modern equipment backed up our

25 Crannog off Port an Eilean, Loch Tummel, drowned when loch raised in 1930s. *Courtesy Gordon Halliwell*

26 The STUA team ready to dive on Loch Tummel crannog off Port an Eilean. *T. Coope*

earlier work in most cases. Most recently, in Spring 2004, we surveyed a major part of the shore of the loch as part of ongoing work by the National Trust for Scotland who are the proprietors of the Lawers range which lies adjacent to the north shore of the loch. As part of this survey we sampled a number of crannogs and obtained materials for environmental analysis and for radiocarbon dating. The results are due in August 2004.

PERTHSHIRE CRANNOG SURVEY

In 2004, a new initiative was set up to examine crannogs elsewhere in Perthshire. This beautiful county has a wide range of geological conditions and the difference in types of lochs reflects this. Some of them are shallow with farmland and natural woodlands while others are deeper often with more barren surroundings. The range is likely to produce crannogs of different forms and possibly different functions. One of the motivations for the new survey was the 350th anniversary of Jean Blaeu's Atlas which includes maps of Scotland. The Scottish element was based on work by Timothy Pont who was one of the first surveyors to map parts of Scotland and his early maps, a fantastic and unique resource, can be accessed through the website of the National Library of Scotland. He noted on his maps places of interest and settlements including a number of islands that, according to the symbols on them, were occupied. These Medieval and later sites are of considerable interest and they are being examined for the first time in some depth by Matthew Shelley, a PhD student at Edinburgh University.

Port an Eilean, Loch Tummel

One of the most interesting sites was drowned in Loch Tummel in 1932 when the loch was raised for a hydro-electric power scheme. The remains of an island that had been inhabited was noted on the early maps and an old photograph showed the position of the site in the loch *(25)*. It was reported as having been the home of Duncan the Stout in the early fourteenth century. He was a member of Clan Donnachie and a supporter of Robert the Bruce. A small team from the STUA located the site using an echo sounder and dived onto exciting remains *(26)*. The island had been covered in trees that were cut down before the island was submerged. The top of the site is now 3m under the water and is covered with the stumps of the cut trees. It was remarkable diving down to land on a well-made flagstone floor with a path leading to a flight of steps that went down to the present loch bed some 2m deeper. Descending the steps into the gloomy depths of the loch was an interesting and unique experience. At the bottom of the flight were a number of timber piles flanking the steps. One of these was sampled for a radiocarbon date.

Loch Monzievaird

A particularly notable site was planned in Loch Monzievaird near the town of Crieff. This site still had many timbers well preserved around the perimeter and underwater there were vertical faces of organic material that looked as if they had

27 Neish's Isle, east end of Loch Earn. N. Dixon

been exposed by collapse sometime in the last few hundred years. The timbers appear to have been placed there to contain and support the outer edge of the island. Samples have been taken for radiocarbon dating.

Neish's Isle, Loch Earn

Other sites were examined in Loch Rannoch, Loch Earn and Loch Drumellie. One of the sites at the east end of Loch Earn, known as Neish's Isle *(27)*, was reputedly the location for a massacre when Smooth John MacNab and 11 of his brothers dragged a boat across the mountains from their home in Loch Tay and beheaded the occupiers of Neish's Isle, apparently for stealing sheep. There are still substantial remains of stone buildings on the island and a very well-formed boat noost, or small harbour. The mound is massive with very large stones down to the loch bed in places more than 4m deep and, like many lochs, is gloomy and dark. There are many timbers lying around on the loch bed but they appear to be mostly modern which is not surprising as this end of the loch is a collecting area for material carried by the currents generated by the prevailing south-westerly winds. Unfortunately, the stone structures on the island are being substantially damaged by campers and fishermen who presumably do not know the importance of this historical site.

It is only possible to list in this book a few of the sites we have examined throughout Scotland. The system for surveying crannogs and other artificial islands is simple and relatively inexpensive. The results are almost invariably exciting and they add important information to the existing archaeological database in Scotland.

Nine

UNDERWATER PRINCIPLES AND PRACTICE

INTRODUCTION

The pros and cons of practising archaeology underwater in general have already been well-covered by a number of publications over the last 40 years (e.g. Bass 1966, UNESCO 1972, UNESCO 1981, Dean *et al* 1992). While the emphasis in past works has been on maritime or nautical archaeology many of the techniques employed and a selection of the tools are directly applicable to the work carried out on sites like Oakbank, albeit with modifications. The underwater methods and techniques discussed below are discussed with special reference to work in shallow waters in inland lochs and particularly to the excavations at Oakbank Crannog. All work there is carried out following the appropriate Health and Safety guidelines.

Acceptance of Underwater Excavation

Until recently, most archaeologists were reluctant to accept the concept of working underwater and for many, even now, the prospect is often not seriously considered. There are a variety of reasons for this even though the practical problems which must be overcome before an underwater excavation is carried out are, in many respects, closely similar to those involved in preparing for a land dig. Background research and survey, administrative issues, organisation of personnel, acquisition of equipment and transport are basically the same in both cases. However, many archeologists still view underwater excavation as more difficult, more expensive or more inaccessible than land excavation, and to many it is simply inconceivable. Fortunately, some heritage agencies have recognised the importance of recording, excavating and preserving underwater sites and new initiatives are including this work in mainstream archaeology, particularly with regard to training, management and protection. This relatively new acceptance of the discipline is also reflected in an increase of postgraduate study programmes available in underwater archaeology such as a new MSc in the subject at Edinburgh University.

EARLY UNDERWATER OBSERVATIONS ON CRANNOGS

Rev. Mapleton and Loch Kielziebar, Argyll

The earliest recorded underwater examination of a crannog in Scotland was carried out by two divers from the Crinan Canal on behalf of the Rev. R.J. Mapleton (Mapleton 1867, 322). The minister had suspected the existence of an artificial island in Loch Kielziebar, near Lochgilphead, Argyll. In 1867 he visited the loch accompanied by the canal engineer 'with a diving apparatus, and a staff of men'. One of the major constraints against working underwater until the invention of the modern aqualung was the amount of equipment required and the number of men needed to operate it. It took two men to turn the hand-operated pump to supply air to the diver and at least two others to handle his air and life-lines. Mapleton's divers seem to have justified their employment, however, it is unacceptable in modern times for an archaeologist to stay on shore and rely upon the observations of archaeological features by untrained divers.

The diving exploits of Rev. Odo Blundell

In the first decade of the twentieth century, the Rev. Francis Odo Blundell from the abbey at Fort Augustus, Inverness-shire became the next person to examine crannogs beneath the surface. In August 1908 in order to establish the artificiality of Eilean Muireach, or Cherry Island, in the west end of Loch Ness, Blundell acquired the use of a diving suit and air pump from the Clyde Navigation Trust who maintained the Caledonian Canal.

He experienced few difficulties after initial problems of too much buoyancy due to over-enthusiastic pumping by his inexperienced assistants. The 'brass-hat' diving suit which he used was heavy and cumbersome and he required a dresser to help him kit up. The air hose and life-line were heavy and care had to be taken not to get them tangled, though this would not have been a great problem in such shallow water. The heavy suit with its pair of 56lb. lead-weighted boots did not allow him to swim free as we can now with modern scuba diving equipment, and he was restricted to walking on the loch bed with the attendant risk of damage to the structure and raising silt which diminished visibility, as he recorded (Blundell 1909, 162).

Even with the restrictions of his antiquated equipment, which incidentally changed little for some work until the 1960s, Blundell recognised through various features the artificial nature of Eilean Muireach: the even pitch of the mound's rubble cover

28 Crannog in Loch Bruiach, near Beauly where Blundell dived using early equipment. *N. Dixon*

and the two layers of stones, large and small; the clearly defined line between the crannog and the loch bed and the range of timbers projecting from the site; the causeway to the shore, a stone breakwater; and a sighting of a mass of vitrified material. The observations he made during his three descents on his first day of diving proved the value of being able to go underwater to examine the site at first hand. This was particularly important during the period when he was working since crannogs had been assigned to the south-west of Scotland due to the impact of Munro's work, except for solely stone mounds in the Highlands. Blundell proved this not to be the case and went on to establish the presence of crannogs with substantial timber elements elsewhere in the Highland lochs.

Blundell followed up his Loch Ness experience with a more arduous visit to Loch Bruiach in the hills above the town of Beauly *(28)*. The loch is isolated and it took considerable efforts to get the diving equipment there with the aid of a horse and cart and a number of strong men. Re-enactment of Blundell's exploits in Loch Ness and Loch Bruiach, for a BBC production, gave first-hand experience of the difficulties of carrying out proper archaeological work with the early equipment.

Blundell put the primitive equipment available to him to its fullest use in terms of underwater archaeology for his day. Even had the desire existed to carry out any more ambitious work, it was not feasible until less bulky and cumbersome equipment had been developed and the only way to reasonably consider excavating an underwater crannog at that time would have begun with draining it. After Blundell's underwater observations there are no records of other divers or archaeologists carrying out the same sort of work until the 1960s, by which time significant changes had taken place in the standards of archaeological excavation and the type of equipment available for working underwater.

Modern underwater equipment
In 1964 and '65 the Islay Archaeological Survey Group surveyed the remains on the island of Inchcailloch in Loch Lomond. As an adjunct to their work an expedition was set up by the British Sub-Aqua Club to establish which, if any, of the numerous islands in the loch were artificially constructed. By this time the ease of transport and the simplicity of the equipment required for diving meant that most Scottish lochs could be examined with little difficulty and crannogs could be surveyed on a scale not previously possible *(colour plate 11)*. The contrast with Blundell's cumbersome efforts at the beginning of the century is dramatic.

In 1972, a systematic survey of Loch Awe was carried out by archaeologists from the University of Edinburgh and a team of Naval Air Command Sub-Aqua Club divers (McArdle *et al* 1973). The supply and handling of the diving gear was carried out mainly by the Naval Air Command Team who also provided nine divers trained in underwater search and survey methods and accustomed to working in low visibility conditions. They supplied two boats with engines and a compressor and air bank, thus taking much of the burden from the scientific members of the team. The discipline and organisation of this experienced group enabled 60 sites to be examined over the 90km of shoreline of Loch Awe in only two weeks. Twenty were confirmed as artificial and were surveyed.

The requirements for underwater survey in terms of equipment are not significantly different from those used in the basic pastime of diving: an air tank, wet or dry suit, weightbelt, mask, fins and snorkel. The survey tools add little to these basic requirements. A compass, which many divers carry anyway, a 30m tape and a 5m telescopic surveyor's staff are adequate for shallow-water survey. More accurate or larger-scale work is carried out using a theodolite or total station from a shore baseline.

THE DEVELOPMENT OF MODERN
UNDERWATER EXCAVATION TECHNIQUES

Dr Ulrich Ruoff, as the archaeologist for the city of Zurich, is the founder of modern underwater excavation techniques for submerged settlements in inland water. He developed these techniques during the excavation of lake-dwellings in the Lake of Zurich beginning in 1963. He established standards which are comparable with land excavation and which others still attempt to achieve. He identified four major areas of difficulty which it is necessary to overcome before accurate and efficient work can be carried out. They are water clarity; recording underwater; communications underwater and conservation.

Water clarity

Disturbance of bottom sediments clouded the water to such an extent that precise work was often impossible. He tried various methods of cleaning the water but eventually devised a new tool. Water is pumped along a hose to a rigid tube 1m long and 5cm in diameter. This tube is perforated along one edge with three rows of holes through which the pumped water is forced thus creating an artificial current. The tube is so placed that excavated material guided into the current is carried away from the working area and the water is kept clear. This tool is widely used on lacustrine sites and is a useful excavation implement at Oakbank Crannog.

Accurate site drawing

Site-drawing was another area where difficulties were encountered by Ruoff. Photogrammetry and general photographic recording cannot supercede drawing in many cases for the same reasons as on land sites, but also because cloudy water can severely restrict light penetration. The importance of viewing vertically an area to be drawn on a land site is well known if distortion is to be avoided in the final plan. The problem is greatly accentuated underwater where parallax, the refraction of light through the water, results in far greater visual aberration. Ruoff pointed out that constant use of a plumb-bob was necessary to minimise errors but developed a less time-consuming method for his own work (Ruoff 1972, 128). He used two grid frames, one above the other, with 5cm separation. Adjustable legs enabled the frames to be horizontally aligned and when viewed from above verticality was assumed if the appropriate grid lines coincided.

Direct reduction of drawings is not an easy operation underwater, particularly when the draughtsman's hands are numb with cold. If gloves are worn to stay warm their bulk makes fine drawing difficult. Ruoff overcame this problem by drawing at 1:1 onto clear plastic sheets which he then photographed on shore. Some of these processes have been modified for use at Oakbank Crannog.

Communications underwater

The difficulty of underwater communications between workers and supervisor was a problem on many underwater excavations. On some sites poor visibility exacerbates the problem as neither workers nor supervisor may be able to see more than small areas at one time. This also makes discussion on shore difficult as specific features cannot be indicated or directly referred to at short notice although in the longer term a video record is a useful tool. In the 1960s, Ruoff attempted to minimise the problem by having a permanent team of three highly trained excavators. Familiarity with the system of operation and with each other meant that verbal communication was kept to a minimum and a higher level of mutual understanding was achieved. This problem is discussed in more detail below with regard to Oakbank Crannog but it is fair to say that it has been mostly overcome with the development of wired and wireless diver communication equipment in the last 20 years.

Conservation

A problem that very soon became apparent to Ruoff was the mass of well-preserved organic material on his sites and the lack of adequate conservation facilities. He overcame this problem by working closely with the Swiss National Museum and encouraged the development of the required experts and services.

A number of other underwater excavations have taken place on the Continent using basically the same techniques pioneered by Ruoff. They include the exciting and important sites of: Tybrind Vig, a Mesolithic site in Denmark (Andersen 1984); a late Neolithic village at Les Baigneurs, Charavines, France (Bocquet 1979); and a palisaded village site in Lake Neuchatel, Switzerland (Delgado 1997, 233).

Ten

METHODS AND TECHNIQUES APPLIED TO OAKBANK CRANNOG

Oakbank Crannog was the first crannog to be excavated underwater from 1980 and work is still being carried out there. Initial work there was to a great extent experimental, the aim being to develop the methods and techniques so that they became a matter of course and could thus be applied to other crannog investigations.

DIVER COMFORT AND SAFETY

As with all archaeological excavations, the site is sacrosanct and is treated with the greatest delicacy and respect. The only compromises made to archaeological rigour at Oakbank are related to diver safety and comfort: safety for the obvious reason that lives are more important than archaeological results and in an alien environment lives are at risk; comfort because the discomfort of those working underwater directly affects the standard of work and the conscientiousness of the workers.

Safety
Diving is a well-regulated business, and the STUA dives under the HSE's *Approved Code of Practice for Scientific and Archaeological Diving Projects* which is part of the Diving at Work Regulations 1997. Compared to deep water sites in the sea, a site which is only 1m below the surface and 20m from the shore can be considered a safe site for underwater archaeology. One of the few dangers of such a site is the shallowness of the water which can tempt even experienced divers to become complacent.

Diving is carried out from a fixed platform built out into the loch so it is immediately beside the site *(colour plate 12)*. Air is supplied by airlines from a surface compressor giving a constant supply that will last as long as the compressor is running. Should it stop unexpectedly, a full cylinder of compressed air cuts in with sufficient capacity to last for about an hour. Divers also carry small 'pony bottles' of compressed air as a totally independent source. Dry suits are worn to combat the cold and allow the divers to stay down for two to three hours at a time. Fins are banned from the site as they can cause damage to the delicate material that is being excavated.

EXCAVATION EQUIPMENT

Oakbank Crannog is effectively a large mound of stones with a core of delicate organic material. The tasks involved in the excavation range from lifting tons of heavy boulders using a range of lifting devices to removing delicate waterlogged wooden artefacts excavated just using a finger tip.

Excavating

A benefit of working on an underwater site is that everything appears about a third bigger than on land so it is easier to see small and complex features or finds. There is no such thing as mud underwater as the water acts as a permanent wetting agent so particles disaggregate easily and finds can be more easily handled, especially when they are of a very fine or delicate nature. Hand tools can be used the same as on land including buckets *(colour plate 13)*, shovels, brushes and trowels *(29)*. The main difference is in the removal of mass materials like sand or gravel. There is no need to shovel these into barrows or bags as they can be moved directly off site.

Grid frames for site control

To ensure that the site is properly and fully recorded a grid frame is often laid down to allow accurate measurements. Strong metal grids let the diver use them for support as well as measuring. They are invaluable for plotting finds and for the alignment of planning frames for site drawing. Consideration must be given to the eventual outcome of such a system since the frames must be either supported or removed when the parts of the site on which they lie are excavated.

Buoyancy as an aid to lifting heavy objects

The buoyancy of air in water is a great benefit to underwater work, particularly when there is a need to move substantial amounts of spoil or stones. Airbags can be filled with air to create massive lift when required. It is not unreasonable to lift five tons underwater, which would require a crane on land.

29 Diver excavating at Oakbank Crannog, Loch Tay. *N. Dixon*

For removing the many large stones that cover Oakbank Crannog to the spoil heaps, a metal platform is suspended beneath a raft. A simple calculation means the weight of stones that can be lifted is known. A gallon of liquid weighs 10 pounds so a 45 gallon oil drum will lift 450 pounds. A raft with four drums can lift 1,800 pounds, almost a ton, minus the weight of the platform to support the stones. The raft is pulled to the stone heaps by an individual sitting on it and the stones are dumped by lowering the platform with a pulley system. The 'dump truck', as it is known, saves the divers from carrying each stone to the stone piles by hand and thus saves an immense amount of time and effort.

Lifting bags

An advantage over dry-land excavation, when moving very large boulders underwater, is to use an air-bag or lifting bag. This is filled with air until the boulder gently rises from the site by the action of the buoyancy in the bag. It is then floated off to the stone dump with no damage to the fragile site and no effort for the diver. The size of weight that can be lifted is only limited by the size of lifting bag available.

Artificial current machine for keeping the water clear

For keeping the water clear of silt and organic debris a current machine was sometimes employed similar to that used by Dr Ruoff (see page 105). A water pump with an output of 600l/min is sited on the platform. It is coupled to a fire hose, leading out to the site, which in turn is coupled to a steel pipe 1m long and 10cm in diameter with a single row of 6mm holes drilled along one edge. A strong current is produced which is easily sufficient to keep the water clear in the immediate area of excavation.

Water dredge for transporting spoil off site

A water dredge, using the same water pump as the current machine, also proves very useful on the site and is the main working tool in most circumstances. The effect of this machine is similar to a vacuum cleaner and a two-person model was developed for use at Oakbank (*colour plate 14*). The excavators hold flexible pipes attached to a long tube leading off the site. Water is pumped through a water jet in the long tube creating suction in the flexible pipes. The excavators feed sand, grit and small stones into the end of the pipe and it is carried along the tube and deposited, neatly sorted, on the loch bed at the edge of the site. The dredge is a relatively gentle machine and is effective without causing damage to the fragile archaeological deposits. The dredge nozzle is never stuck into the site, instead the material is gently broken up by hand and wafted into the end of the pipe.

Hand-fanning for controlled excavation

Most of the actual excavation and cleaning of layers is accomplished by hand-fanning. A fanning motion of the flattened hand can cause very violent or very gentle currents in the water as required and is used for disturbing and transporting most types of material. In well-compacted deposits a trowel may have to be used, and the whole range of dry-site excavation tools may be useful, but only as an adjunct to fanning. Students invariably find it amusing when they are told about the range of hand-fanning techniques and are encouraged to practice the different methods. The whole hand is very powerful and can make the spoil move in different ways depending on the actions used while a single finger can be used to very delicately excavate even the most fragile of finds.

FINDS PROCESSING

One of the practical aspects of working on Oakbank Crannog that requires constant ingenuity and careful consideration is the handling and raising of the many delicate objects discovered during excavation. Any object, except inorganic material, such as stones, will be only slightly negatively buoyant when excavated and unless it is contained will be transported easily by water movements too slight to be readily apparent. Therefore finds must be kept in enclosed containers, fastened down or taken directly to shore. Because the finds come in all sorts of shapes and sizes it is essential to have a wide range of containers available. The range usually includes dairy produce and ice-cream containers, plastic plumbing pipe of various diameters for long thin objects that are the most vulnerable, plastic fertiliser bags for non-crucial timbers, water cisterns and storage tanks for more precious large timbers and sample bags of all different sizes. Planks and builder's polythene, used to make custom-sized containers for particularly awkward timbers, are also available on shore.

A great deal of material from the site cannot justifiably be treated as individually recorded small finds but is still regarded as worthy of collection. This includes scattered burnt bone, some nuts and seeds, woodchips and undifferentiated debris. Each excavator has a plastic box which contains polythene bags labelled for different groups of material into which unplanned finds are placed. The selection is discretionary and may be questioned but is justified on the grounds that a final decision on acceptance or rejection of a particular object is best made in more relaxed conditions on shore. This material is a problem as it is of incidental importance but costs a lot to conserve. However, unless some of it is kept it will not be represented in the final record of the site except on paper.

Artefacts whose position is to be recorded are placed in a finds bag with a drafting-film tag on which is written the find's location, context and description. The bag is

30 Tray full of finds kept underwater for protection during Oakbank Crannog excavation. *N. Dixon*

fastened with a clothes peg to a plastic washing line attached to a tray like those used by bakers for carrying bread *(30)*. The tray is kept underwater until the end of the working session so the finds are given as much protection as possible from the point where they are released from the organic matrix that has stabilised them for thousands of years. A find's position is plotted immediately by triangulation on two tapes attached to the corner control point of the appropriate area. All finds are kept in wet storage until conservation, drying out or discarding is eventually decided upon.

Large finds (such as timbers presumed to be structural but with no marks of having been worked) are reburied in the loch-bed sediments near to shore and are left underwater for future research requirements. Similar timbers of a smaller size are stored in the same place in heavy-duty plastic sacks.

Delicate finds or those of particular interest are treated as dictated by their condition and position when found and are taken directly to shore when excavated. Very fragile finds are embedded in sand to prevent movement before being taken to shore. An element of discretion is therefore essential in handling all of the waterlogged wooden objects from the site, as even large apparently strong timbers have the consistency of hard cheese and will not support their own weight.

There are advantages in the observation and examination of finds underwater. Objects underwater are usually very clean when discovered with little material adhering to them. Since they have not been exposed to oxygen or light for a great deal of time, when first exposed they retain their original freshness but regrettably this fades very quickly and within half-an-hour the freshness of colour is faded to a dull grey. Since this is never recovered finds are photographed as soon after exposure as possible.

SURVEYING, PLANNING AND DRAWING

Laying out semi-permanent control points to enable general survey of the site is not much more difficult than on land and is actually sometimes easier since the surrounding loch bed is clear of obstructions and easy to penetrate. There are no animals or human interference to move the pegs from year to year. Plastic or metal pegs are advised since the buoyancy of wooden ones tends to draw them slowly from the bottom silts. The pegs can be used for tape triangulation but obviously not for theodolite positioning since they are two or more metres deep.

The normal use of tapes for offset planning and triangulation pose few difficulties underwater so long as the visibility is sufficient to see the tape along its entirety *(31)*. Constant checks have to be made to ensure that it has not snagged on stones or weeds but this is no more of a problem than on a land site. Basic planning and drawing underwater are made more difficult than on land because of wave action and the difficulties of working in diving gear, however, the same level of accuracy can be achieved as on land.

The best method of planning the site for speed and accuracy is the total station. The machine is sited safely in the dry *(colour plate 15)*. In water up to 5m deep the diver acts as staffman *(32)* and a snorkeller is required to pass messages from the machine operator on shore to the diver underwater. The staff held by the diver has a prism attached to the upper end, which reflects an infra-red beam back to the machine on shore giving a highly accurate distance and angle reading very quickly.

Site planning and the problem of parallax
There are no constraints to drawing sketch plans, recording and note-taking underwater so long as work is not hampered by bad weather. In the early days writing boards were made by roughening white perspex with sand paper but now a variety of simple plastic notepads are available in dive shops. Plastic drafting film is not affected by immersion and can be used for writing or drawing on site.

A problem encountered underwater, that is not experienced on land, is that of parallax, as recognised by Ruoff. The different refractive index of water means that visual distortion is obvious when trying to observe the angle and distance

31 Measuring in finds at Oakbank Crannog. *STUA*

32 Holding staff for planning crannog with total station on shore. *B.L. Andrian*

33 Drawing part of Oakbank Crannog at full-scale onto plastic sheets. *B.L. Andrian*

between different objects or features. While this is not normally an issue it makes drawing detailed plans more difficult because of the visual distortion. Planning is also difficult because of the extra level of concentration required and the relative difficulty of seeing through a diving mask.

At Oakbank, the usual land method of planning by laying a 1m square grid, with intersecting string at 20cm intervals, on the area to be drawn and reducing the drawing directly onto a board is difficult unless the water is very calm and the area to be drawn is simple. Even with a double-strung drawing frame, the problem of parallax is always present.

The problems of planning the site are partly overcome by drawing at full-scale on clear plastic sheets underwater *(33)* with the more detailed 1:10 reduction done on shore *(34)*. A conveyor-belt system is set up where the diver draws the first square metre of site with black oil crayon on the clear plastic board and hands the completed drawing up to be reduced on shore. The diver then draws the next square on a second board. The first drawing is reduced onto the master plan on shore and an assistant cleans the board and delivers it back to the diver who hopefully will have completed the next part of the drawing, and so on.

Using this method it takes about 20 minutes to draw each square metre of site. Since the usual trench size is 5m x 5m there are 25 drawings to be made taking

34 Reducing underwater drawing from Oakbank Crannog on shore. N. Dixon

about eight-and-a-half hours or a day's work underwater. This is the most difficult task on the Oakbank excavation, both time-consuming and strenuous, and it needs to be done every time sufficient excavation has taken place to change the site. Normally, in a four-week excavation the site will be fully planned two or three times. Considerable thought has gone into trying to develop a quicker and easier method, such as photographing the board instead of drawing it, but no satisfactory alternative has been found. One of the main benefits of the method is that every detail of the site is guaranteed to be closely examined by the draftspersons below and above the water surface.

VISUAL RECORDING AND GRAPHIC PRESENTATION OF SUBMERGED CRANNOGS

As a result of their location in or under water, crannogs are not readily visible to the casual observer. Even those which project above the water surface as islands often have a different shape and form below water level, as can be seen in the cases of Eilean nam Breaban and Croftmartaig Island in Loch Tay. Both of these crannogs appear as small, roughly circular islands when observed from the shore but surveyed plans and aerial photographs show a very different shape underwater. In the case of submerged sites not only can they not be observed from shore but even divers underwater do not perceive their whole outline owing to the large size of the mounds and the peatiness of the water, and because the angle of viewing is necessarily very low. The same restriction applies to large areas undergoing excavation and to extensive features which might not be recognised as such when seen piecemeal.

A number of techniques have been tried to represent the crannog at Oakbank as realistically as possible. In some cases the intention was to display the whole site and in others to show elements exposed during excavation. The methods used range from aerial photography to computer graphics. The particular situation underwater may prevent the use of certain techniques. For instance, the depth of a site may prevent aerial photography through the water surface. The attempt to present the site as a whole is not only for the benefit of the excavators but is also seen as important in clarifying the form of crannogs for other archaeologists who cannot venture underwater.

Aerial photography

For locating submerged crannogs and for presenting a general picture of shape and size, aerial survey can be very useful. Sites in Loch Tay and elsewhere have been photographed from the air on a number of occasions from both helicopters and fixed-wing aircraft. Helicopters are particularly useful since the steep shores of the lochside offer few emergency landing facilities for fixed-wing aircraft.

The overall image of the sites can be very good, in some cases exhibiting the shadow of the lowest boulders on the loch bed in over 3m of water *(35)*. However, a full outline of the sites is rarely clear as the shadow of the mound obscures the lower edge of the crannogs on the side furthest from the sun and if the sun is hidden by clouds it is difficult to see the stones in detail. Wind-generated ripples on the surface obscure and distort smaller features and where the site is too deep it does not show up at all through the water. Aerial survey is valuable in confirming the general shape of sites which can be planned more accurately from the shore and for supplying an overall impression of the sites. So far, no extensive flights have been made specifically to record crannogs and other submerged sites. If special efforts are made to use polarising filters on cameras, to choose the best weather conditions, sunshine with no wind and to fly at the optimum height, then very useful results can be expected.

One of the main problems of aerial survey is, of course, the expense of hiring a suitable aircraft. Elsewhere, balloons and airfoil kites have been used successfully for low-level aerial work and model aircraft, with floats so they can take off from the water, are also a real possibility for convenience and lower cost.

35 *Above* Crannog off Fearnan, Loch Tay showing penetration of water in good light conditions. *M. Brooks*

36 *Opposite* Contour plan of Oakbank Crannog. *I.W. Morrison*

Subjective planning

The 1979 Loch Tay crannog survey employed a tape and staff method of planning the sites which was simple and relatively accurate and the same method is employed today for quick plans. It is subjective in that the staffman has to decide where the sloping sides of the stone mound level off and become the top working area and which arrangements of stones constitute features. An important benefit is the familiarity which the surveyor develops with the details of the site.

Computer-drawn, objective contour survey

During the 1979 Loch Tay survey Oakbank Crannog was planned more comprehensively than the other sites in an effort to gain more objectivity and accuracy. The loch was calm and the water level was used as the datum. A tape was strung from a theodolite on shore to an inflatable boat, which

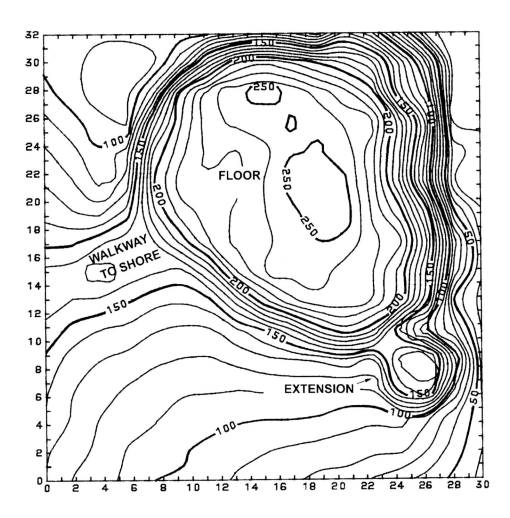

was kept in position on the theodolite crosshairs. A diver with a staff took a depth reading every 2m along the tape. The theodolite was then moved 2m to the side and the depth readings were continued. Altogether 256 readings were taken over the site. Eventually a square grid of depth readings taken every 2m covered the site. They were used as data for a computer graphics programme which produced the contour plan *(36)*. The result is an accurate representation of the irregular main mound with the extension on the west and the low ridge of the causeway remains running off to the north.

The problems of this method are all related to the practical survey. A minimum of four people was required to operate the equipment and the project took a day-and-a-half to complete. It was fortunate that the weather conditions were calm and sunny but such a situation could not be relied upon. The theodolite had to be set up 16 times on slippery boulders and a skilled operator was required to handle it and another to drive the outboard-engined inflatable, however, it is now possible to achieve the same results with fewer readings of a more random nature. Using modern laptop computers linked to the total station the plans, including contours, of a site can be drawn as the readings are taken.

Three-dimensional computer projection

One of the most useful outcomes of the close-contour plot was the creation of three-dimensional projections of the crannog *(37)*. Views with and without an over-emphasised vertical exaggeration have proved useful. The image can be viewed from any direction and the line of sight can be depressed or elevated. The over-emphasised vertical element exaggerates features of the site so that they are more obvious than in the normal view and are more readily distinguished while the unemphasised projection is more realistic. At Oakbank Crannog, the ridge of remains representing the walkway to the shore is much easier to see on the three-dimensional projection. The relationship between the main crannog and the extension is also emphasised and an obvious dip in the top of the site over the area of the floor layer in B3 is also clear. Underwater, because of visibility and parallax problems these features are much more difficult to discern.

As in the case of the contour plan a good visual image is produced, however it is misleading since the computer programme 'rounds-off' sharp breaks in slope thereby suppressing the desirable subjective elements recognised by the planners. In particular, the change between the crannog's stony bottom edge and the flat, light-coloured loch-bed silts is very obvious in fact but is smoothed out by the programme. A combination of the computer's versatility in presenting and storing different views of the site but incorporating breaks in slope and other features are more representative and are now achievable

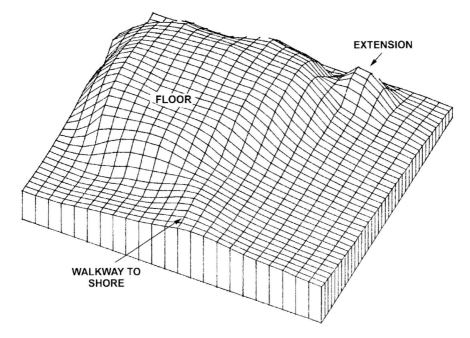

37 Three-dimensional view of Oakbank Crannog based on close contour survey. *I.W. Morrison*

with modern equipment. The Oakbank projections were produced in the early 1980s when computer hardware and software was much more primitive.

Photography

The above methods have been used at Oakbank Crannog to represent the site as an entity but it is also necessary to illustrate parts of the site prior to and during excavation. Planning and drawing of excavated areas is carried out as on land for the detailed recording of the site but photography plays a greater role in most underwater excavations and is particularly useful at Oakbank. The photographs are not just for record purposes but also to demonstrate to those who cannot dive the nature of the site and the work being carried on there.

The texture and colour of the organic matrix may be shown, to a certain degree, by colour photographs. On first being uncovered wood, seeds, bracken, nuts and other organic finds are the same fresh colour as that of new material but within 30 minutes or so the intensity of the colour has faded until eventually a dark charcoal grey is reached with no evidence of the original freshness. In the case of artefacts the effect can be dramatic as in the photographs of a wooden plate in situ *(38)* and after conservation *(52)*.

In the past, there was a delay between photographing the site and seeing the results but now one of the benefits of digital cameras is that the results are instantaneous and shots can be retaken until they are satisfactory.

38 Wooden plate newly excavated, before colour fades. *N. Dixon*

Photomosaics

Unfortunately, the technique of creating photomosaics to show a complete picture of a whole site in gloomy conditions underwater, often used very successfully in representing whole shipwrecks, is not very satisfactory on crannogs due to the fact that the depth of water over the top of the site is not sufficient to allow an adequate distance between camera and subject. This means that a very wide-angle lens has to be used to cover a reasonable area resulting in unacceptable distortion in all except the centre of the frame. A better result could be achieved on deeper parts of the site or by carrying out the operation in winter when the water is 1.5-2.0m deeper, thus enabling a less distorting perspective to be used. Efforts have been made using stills taken from a video scan but they are not much more useful although the video is more effective as a part of the overall site record.

Practical model building

One of the most frustrating aspects to develop during excavation at Oakbank is the lack of immediately perceptible order or pattern in the large number of piles exposed. Except for a few obvious features it is very difficult to make sense of the mass of timbers on the site. This is due to three main reasons. First, more than one phase of building accounts for the piles and stakes and, since the tops of them are eroded to a common level, it is not possible to distinguish the different phases without total excavation or the use of laboratory techniques. This means that a much greater number of uprights than would have been extant during occupation are being observed together. Second, many of the uprights are sloping, presumably mainly because of structural collapse, and they do not appear in their original positions when first observed. This situation becomes less confusing as excavation proceeds and the direction and angle of slope can be used to work out the original position of the point. Third, the impracticability of observing all the timbers at once and the poor visibility underwater make it impossible to view the area as a whole.

The situation is slightly clearer when the site plans and sections are referred to but part of the problem is that the drawings try to represent in two dimensions what is a three-dimensional area with piles standing up to a metre high. In one case it was decided to make a simple three-dimensional model based on the site plans with sticks in the positions where it was decided the uprights had been placed rather than where they now lay. The extrapolated positions were to a certain extent subjective, since the bottoms of many uprights have not yet been excavated, but the results clearly demonstrate a more coherent view of the structure *(39)*. The model was particularly useful for breaking down preconceived groupings based on early observations of the tops of piles and for indicating associations which had not been previously considered. It also emphasised areas in which greater care in recording and examination were required such as an accurate determination of the direction and angle of

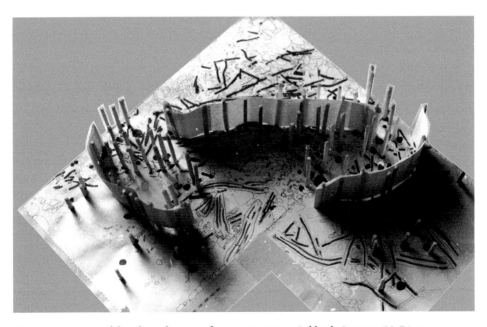

39 Interpretative model to show elements of entry structure at Oakbank Crannog. *N. Dixon*

the slope of uprights which would allow more accurate calculations of their original positions before complete excavation *(colour plate 16)*.

The reconstruction of the entrance with flanking walls, outside walkway supports, internal roof supports and a partition screening the floor area from the outside was only appreciated by examination of the model. Not all of the timbers indicated in it were necessarily contemporary, as had been shown above by the different levels of penetration of the site, but in many cases the later uprights were erected to strengthen weakened earlier ones thus establishing a contact between different chronological phases of occupation. The sequence of building and rebuilding on the crannog will eventually be established by dendrochronology or archaeological recording and the model will then be useful for demonstrating that sequence, by removal or insertion of the sticks. Now the same effect may be produced by computer but 3D computer imaging software is complicated and really needs the assistance of a skilled operator. For the first time, in 2004, a post-graduate student at Edinburgh University, Rosa Mendosa Roble, is using elements of Oakbank Crannog to create a three-dimensional model which can be used to interpret features that are not clear on the two-dimensional drawings.

SUMMARY

A number of methods of illustrating the crannog at Oakbank have been outlined above. Some are traditional and others less so, but all have been found useful to some degree in presenting the site as a whole, or in part, or in exhibiting certain aspects of the work being carried out there. Over the years many methods of displaying Oakbank Crannog have been attempted but none is as compelling as the full-scale crannog built in Loch Tay.

It would have been inconceivable for archaeologists prior to the second half of the twentieth century to consider carrying out excavations underwater. The value of observations beneath the surface was appreciated by Blundell but the weight of the diving equipment and its unwieldy nature in use prevented effective work.

Modern equipment and techniques of working underwater have removed many of the difficulties of early research and Scottish crannogs can now be examined at the convenience of the archaeologist and not only when they are exposed as a result of other work. Exploitation of these sites to the highest archaeological standards is now possible and the mass of important data which they contain is available for systematic research.

Eleven

UNDERWATER EXCAVATIONS AT OAKBANK CRANNOG, LOCH TAY

Excavation has taken place intermittently since 1980 and in that time a total of 68 weeks was spent on site. It may help to understand the structural issues discussed in this chapter by referring to the site grid plan *(40)*. The early work at Oakbank, from 1980 to 1983, makes up the major part of the author's PhD thesis (Dixon 1984).

It is instructive to survey crannogs around the country, but there comes a time when it is necessary to go further to establish a greater depth of knowledge about the sites. The next logical step is excavation, and work at the site of Oakbank Crannog has proved highly productive in explaining the structure of that site and the way of life of the people who lived there. Obviously, limited excavation of a selection of sites can only clarify certain elements of their structure and more work is needed but what has been carried out so far has been useful in laying down ground rules for further research and for showing what might be expected from similar submerged sites.

This book is not the place to go into great depth on the detailed scientific analyses that have come about from the Oakbank excavation. A number of researchers have been involved over the years and their contributions have been invaluable in helping to decode the site. Where appropriate they will be referred to in the text and their publications and dissertations are listed at the end on pages 185-86.

'Oakbank' is named after the cottage of that name located near the crannog in the village of Fearnan, four-and-a-half miles from Kenmore, on the north

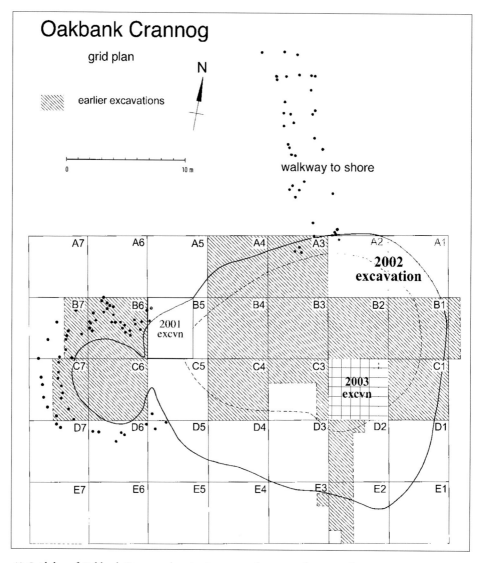

40 Gridplan of Oakbank Crannog showing important features and excavated areas.

shore of Loch Tay. There were a number of good archaeological and practical reasons for choosing this site for excavation over any of the other 17 crannogs in the loch.

REASONS FOR CHOOSING OAKBANK CRANNOG

Archaeologically the site showed a great deal of potential as timbers were exposed and the odd shape suggested that the crannog had a complex structural history. Superficially it appears to be a mound of boulders rising from a flat, sandy loch bed which slopes slightly down from north to south, away from the shore. The crannog mound stands about 1.5m proud of the loch bed nearest the shore and about 3.5m high on the offshore side. The top of the site is never less than 1.5m underwater in summer, while in winter it may be up to 3m underwater.

Shape

In plan it is roughly pear-shaped with the narrow end to the west and the wide end to the east. Adjoining the west end is a sub-circular extension with the superficial appearance of a low mound of boulders resembling a very small, almost independent, crannog. The top of the small mound is considerably lower, and therefore deeper underwater, than the top of the main mound suggesting that it was not a living platform in the same manner as the crannog proper.

The two mounds are joined with a narrow neck of large boulders and the loch bed on the north or landward side of the neck is almost 1m higher than on the south side because of silt build-up. Prior to excavation, on the south-east edge of the extension, four evenly-spaced pile stumps of a softish wood were visible with a number of horizontal timbers of the same wood interspersed haphazardly among them *(41)*. Later work showed there were two concentric circles of piles around this part of the site. Near the edge of the crannog, but

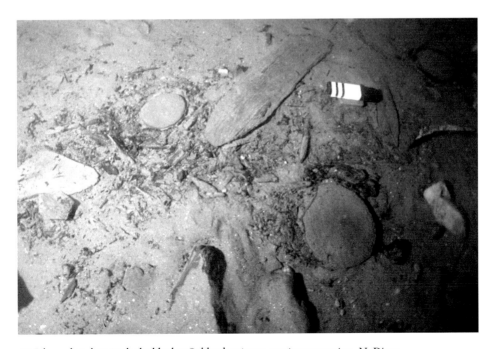

41 Piles and timbers in the lochbed at Oakbank prior to starting excavation. N. Dixon

close to the other timbers, was the stump of an oak pile embedded in the loch bed. This was sampled and gave a radiocarbon date of 460±60 BC (GU-1325). Initially, the layout of piles in this area seemed haphazard but later examination showed that the evenly-spaced soft wood piles were only part of an arrangement of 70 piles which surrounded the extension.

Leading from the north edge of the main site into the shallows there is a low ridge on the loch bed. Along the length of this ridge, and projecting from it, are the stumps of 40 oak and elm piles. Some horizontal timbers were observed projecting from beneath the crannog at the south end of the ridge and from the boulders in the shallows at the north end. Clearly these are the remains of a walkway from the crannog to the shore.

Later examination of the walkway showed that it stops just short of the shore leaving a gap of about 2m. There are four piles in the loch bed across the end of the walkway and it is most likely that there was a gate across the end. This theory is supported by the discovery of a row of small pile points in the loch bed running parallel to the shore from the end of the walkway to the west and to the east, presumably supporting a fence in the shallow water to prevent access to the site. Clearly defence began at the shore end of the walkway and not on the crannog itself.

Entrance to the crannog

On the top of the crannog around control point A3 a number of irregular oak timbers were observed possibly representing the remains of an entrance. Nearby were the tops of two piles: one of oak and the other alder. The larger oak pile (103) was sampled for radiocarbon dating and eventually produced a date of 595±55 BC (GU-1323). Around the base of the radiocarbon-dated sample a deposit of organic material was observed and a preliminary examination revealed cereal, grass and a wide variety of well-preserved seed types.

The substantial amounts of organic material in the form of timbers and plant debris, along with the well-defined morphological features of the crannog, extension and causeway are not all found on the other sites in Loch Tay. Oakbank Crannog was accordingly selected for excavation with a degree of confidence in the prospect of uncovering more well-preserved organic features and deposits within the mound, underlying the cover of boulders.

As this was the first underwater excavation of a crannog, practical considerations also played a role in the choice of Oakbank Crannog. Permission to set up a field office and equipment base in a field beside the shore was given by the landowners who have given tremendous support ever since. The site is adjacent to the main road that runs along the north shore of the loch and accommodation, post office, general store and hotel were all within a few yards of the site *(colour plate 17)*.

The underwater conditions were equally favourable. The loch-bed silt is not too fine and so it is relatively easy to keep the water clear even with a considerable element of disturbance during excavation The water is clean and visibility is generally very good except in turbulent storms or after periods of heavy rain.

THE EXCAVATION

Overlying stones

A layer of large boulders, ranging in size from 30-80cm, covers and surrounds the site and the first task in 1980 was to remove these stones from a small trench laid out on the top of the site. These boulders are a consistent feature of almost all of the Highland crannogs and their presence was an issue that needed explanation. At first, it was not clear whether they were scattered randomly throughout the makeup of the mound at Oakbank. It was with some surprise that the layer of stones on top of the site was seen to be in some places only two or three stones deep, although they were up to 3m deep around the edges possibly to protect the site from wave action.

The thin layer of boulders overlying the area on top of the mound is also difficult to explain. If it had been laid before a structural timber phase, possibly to raise the overall level of the site, it would then be impossible to drive stakes into the underlying material. The resulting stony mound would support a stone structure, but no remains of foundations were found to indicate such a structure had existed. It seemed likely therefore that the stones were laid after the insertion of upright wooden stakes to help consolidate them during a later construction phase.

Underlying the layer of large boulders was a layer of smaller, roughly fist-sized stones. They had the appearance of having been deliberately laid down, possibly as a firm base for the upper stones to lie on. However, there is no evidence to prove contemporaneity of the two deposits. The smaller stones overlay a thin covering (1-5cm) of grit and silt with very small stone chips which is probably the result of degradation of the upper layers and natural deposition of waterborne silt and requires no explanation in terms of human involvement.

Removing the stones is an exhausting task but gives the excavators a chance to get used to working in the shallow waters and to become accustomed to the site. Stone dumps were established around the perimeter of the mound and originally each stone was carried to these dumps by hand. It may not have been the most exciting work but it certainly developed the fitness of the team. Since 1980 we have moved many tons of stones to these dumps that now surround the site like a range of small mountains.

Organic Matrix

Immediately underlying the upper, stony layers is a deposit of organic material which, given the height of the mound, must be 3m thick in places *(colour plate 16)*. While organic material had already been sampled from the site prior to excavation, there had been no suspicion of the range and richness of the debris. It included: upright stakes and more substantial piles, some more or less vertical and others sloping steeply; longitudinal branches and timbers, some in clearly associated groups and others of a single, random nature; compacted plant debris consisting mainly of bracken and fern stems, twigs, straw, leaves and animal excreta, insect remains; and a wide range of seeds and nuts.

This mass of organic debris initially gave the impression of being one massive layer but excavation proved that it is made up of many lenses of compacted material. Upper lenses can be peeled from those underneath occasionally with a seam of insect puparia, seeds or animal droppings marking the boundary between them. In other cases the distinct strata are accentuated by different alignments of bracken laid down as bedding material. Sometimes more random deposits are encountered such as, concentrations of wood chips, coarse sawdust, fibrous bracken stems and straw or soft and creamy dung-like material. In some cases these layers are compressed to less than 1cm thick.

Being used to uncovering dark patches of soil representing postholes and pits on land sites, it is a revelation to be confronted with the materials as if they had just been gathered from the landscape. In the first excavation season it became immediately apparent that this would be a very different sort of excavation and that there was effectively no 'spoil'. Everything on the site looked as fresh as when it had been deposited by the people who once lived there. It is not possible to recover and analyse cubic tons of this material so selection of specific areas or deposits is critical; almost everything has some archaeological value and contains information about the local environment and its exploitation.

Timbers and structural features

For an archaeologist used to the postholes of land excavation there is something particularly exciting about excavating and handling the actual timbers cut down by the crannog-builders *(42)*. Most of the timbers still have the bark on them and often the stumps of small branches and twigs that have been trimmed off are still there. The majority of piles are alder with some oak, elm and the occasional willow. Smaller pieces are generally hazel and birch. Some have cutmarks and obvious evidence of working while others seem to have been dragged in straight from the woods. When the exposure of one timber leads to others in close proximity obviously representing a complex feature, then the uncovering of that feature brings home the true thrill of archaeological discovery.

42 Piles with organic matrix removed. *N. Dixon*

The wooden elements of the site are mostly embedded in the deep layer of organic debris and owe their excellent state of preservation to that deposit. Where timbers project from the organic matrix they are eroded back to the surface of the deposit. Only oakwood survives in open water and even here the bark and sapwood are eroded away and only the heartwood survives. The heartwood becomes what is commonly termed 'bog oak' and is harder than fresh new oak. Timbers and other organic remains are also well preserved in the silts of the loch bed but they are eroded to the level of the silt surface. Certainly the standard of preservation of plant and insect material protected by the organic matrix is very high. Vivid examples are the discovery of a wild cherry complete with its flesh and sheep droppings with parasite eggs preserved in them.

Threshold timber

One of the most important structural finds to date was a large, complex beam with holes cut through it *(43)*. This has been interpreted as the threshold timber of the entrance, although it may possibly have been a lintel instead. The threshold would be the timber that was stepped over to get through the door while the lintel would be the timber over the door. There is a considerable element of speculation as to how the timber was actually used and, according to the number, size and arrangement of holes, it is possible that it was a timber re-used from an earlier function. There is not space here to go into the full range of speculations but the timber may have served as a base for the construction of hazel hurdles or wall panels, and was then reused later as a part of the entrance structure. It is notable that it is more complex than anything that has been used in the modern reconstruction and indicates the skill and sophistication of the carpenters on the original crannog.

Hazel rods

Overlying the threshold timber was a bundle of long thin hazel rods of the sort that would be used to make hurdles for walls and fences *(colour plate 19)*. They may have been stored there for later use or perhaps they had been laid down to cover up an uneven part of the floor or fill a gap between floor timbers. Similar hazel withies were discovered on a deeper part of the site in the extension to the west of the main mound.

Uprights

The hundreds of stakes and piles on the site range between 5cm and 45cm in diameter, with the majority around 10-15cm *(44)*. Most of the wooden uprights in the main crannog mound are the remains of structural features which had different functions on the platform. Straight lines of stakes may represent the preserved

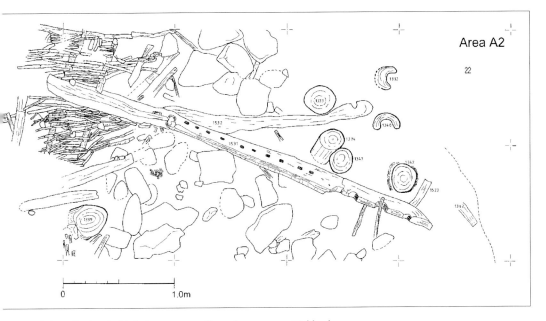

43 Possible threshold timber among collapsed structure at Oakbank.

44 Small alder and oak piles exposed during excavation at Oakbank. *N. Dixon*

elements of partition walls and dividers inside the house. Curved and circular arrangements around the edge of the mound may have supported an unroofed walkway around the outside of the house and may also have supported a stockade at the outer edge of the walkway. Other curves of piles and stakes, further in from the edge, may show the line of the outside wall of the house and may also have supported a ring beam to take the strain of the roof-poles.

While these ideas may seem reasonable and logical, one of the biggest problems is trying to establish which uprights go together as parts of a feature. They all look alike but may have been driven in during building or repairs at any time in a 200-year period. This is one of the most important issues on the site since only by assigning timbers to specific common groups is it possible to create the elements that made up the dwelling in the many different phases of occupation.

The stakes and piles excavated so far all show evidence of having been cut to a point at the lower end to facilitate driving them into the organic matrix or the loch-bed silts. In some cases cutting could be seen at the place where the stake projected from the organic material. These stakes were only set into the matrix to the level of the facets of the cut point and are clearly evidence of secondary construction on the site since the organic matrix must have been laid down prior to their insertion. A number of small stake points were discovered on the uppermost part of the site and two were sent for radiocarbon dating. They produced dates of 410±60 BC (GU-1463) and 455±60 BC (GU-1464). Because they were just the points of stakes, the upper parts having been completely eroded away, they must be some of the last stakes used on the site and so are of particular importance. In fact, no later dates have come from the site.

It is interesting to note that one of the earliest radiocarbon dates from the site came from the top of an oak pile, with a date of 595±55 BC (GU-1323), not far from the two small stakes. This may seem strange but as the two stakes were just sticking into the top of the organic matrix and the oak goes all the way through it, probably into the loch bed itself, they all played a part in the structure at the same time. The difference is that the oak was a major structural timber helping to hold up the house for the whole life of the crannog while the stakes were just introduced towards the end.

The range of radiocarbon dates from Oakbank is informative. All of the dates fall into two main areas of time which are around 400-450 BC and around 550-600 BC. Unfortunately, because of a problem in the calibration curve for this period, the range of dates when calibrated is from about 800 BC to about 300 BC. As there are a number of calibration methods available, the dates in this book are left uncalibrated, unless otherwise stated. The list of dates shows where the samples that were analysed came from (see page 178).

The house floor

Longitudinal timbers exposed in the excavated areas ranged from the remains of hurdles of around 2cm in diameter to large structural pieces of up to 40cm in diameter. The most coherent groups are those which make up the internal upper floor *(46, 47)*, and those of the underlying floor foundations. The floors at Oakbank Crannog are possibly the largest areas of preserved timber floor from the Iron Age in Britain and are particularly impressive as they were still covered by the layers of bracken and fern laid down by the crannog-dwellers. The close association and superficial appearance of the timbers in these two groups suggest that they were taken from the same stands of trees which may have been the results of coppicing. The upper timbers in particular were all of similar diameter and were straight stems up to 4m long with little evidence of side branches. The lower layer was made up of smaller branches with less regularity than those overlying them, but with similar diameters within the group.

Although a number of the upper floor timbers have been flattened on the upper surface this is not deliberate and is the result of natural erosion. There were three layers of timbers making up the floor and the lower ones were roundwood with no upper flattening. The eroded surfaces were covered by the upper layers of silt and stone and seem to have been degraded prior to deposition of the boulders.

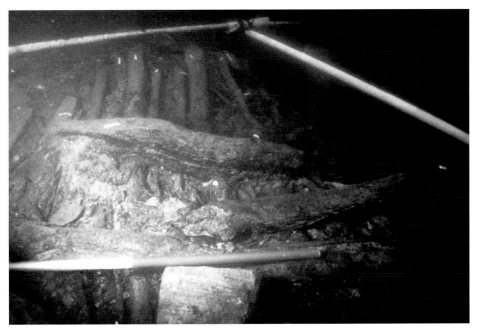

46 Main floor in Area C2, Oakbank Crannog. *B.L. Andrian*

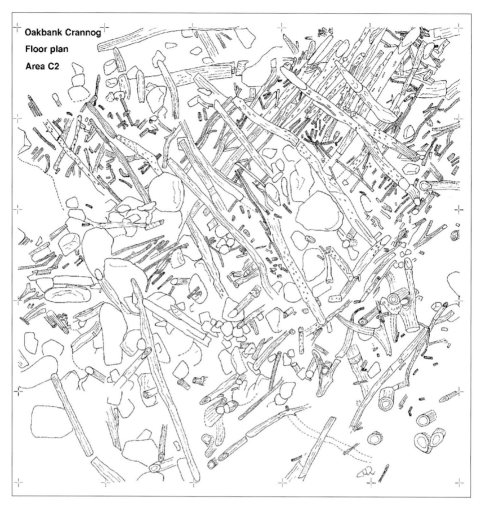

47 Floorplan of main floor in Area C2.

The first floor remains were uncovered in 1981, in Area B3, but a bigger area came to light in 1990, in Area C2, when the remains of fallen uprights were also discovered lying across the floor. The 1990 section is sloping into Area C1, towards the outside of the east side of the site and seems to have collapsed down in that direction.

Floor foundation

The exposed floor was backfilled with silt over a net cover to protect it until we could return to continue the excavation there, which resumed in 2003 with exciting results. Important elements of the floor foundation were uncovered including the remains of broken piles in association with many other timbers that

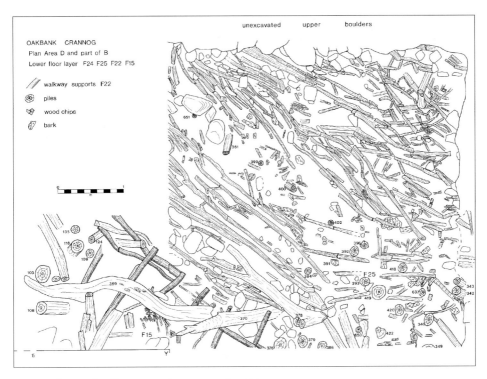

48 Foundation of walkway around crannog in Area B3.

are part of the period of habitation immediately preceding the construction of the floor. Other structural timbers in Area B3 represent the foundation of the floor there and also of part of the walkway around the house *(48)*. Six radially aligned beams, 7-8cm in diameter and roughly 50cm apart, are crossed at around 90° by other transverse timbers.

ACCURATE RECORDING

The mass of material remaining at Oakbank Crannog means that it is possible to reconstruct with great detail many aspects of the structure and the way of life of the inhabitants. The site was inhabited for a considerable period of time, 200 years or more according to the radiocarbon dates, and it was repaired and rebuilt a number of times. Clear evidence of different phases of collapse and repair were seen with the excavation of a large wooden bowl from an abandonment layer that had had a large pile driven through it during later rebuilding *(colour plate 20)*. So far, almost 2,000 major timbers have been recorded on the site and many thousands of smaller pieces of wood have been observed but not recorded in detail. It is very difficult to work out the different phases of occupation and building on the crannog, so detailed and accurate recording is needed to help the interpretation.

49 Timber jumble and collapsed structure at Oakbank. *B.L. Andrian*

TIMBER STRUCTURES

In some cases, the groups of timbers represent obvious features, such as the two areas of flooring discovered so far. In other cases the arrangement of timbers does not make for easy recognition of features but if the timbers are all accurately recorded it may be possible to reconstruct elements after interpretation. For example, the floor timbers along with the small stakes beside them and the lack of upright piles on each side of the partition clearly suggests an entrance area and the inner floor of the house. Even very confusing jumbles of timbers *(49)* must still be fully and accurately recorded as their purpose may become clear with future excavation.

TOOLMARK SIGNATURE MATCHING

One of the most exciting elements of the well-preserved piles uncovered at Oakbank, were the very obvious ridges and grooves on the facets of the cut points *(45)*. They were made by notches or roughness on the cutting edge of the axe or adze used to shape them. It seemed that some of the patterns of ridges and grooves were the same on different timbers suggesting that they had been cut using the same tool. Effectively the signature that was noted was like a fingerprint unique to a single tool.

45 Toolmark signature on pile at Oakbank. *B.L. Andrian*

In 1988 a student was given six piles from Oakbank to see if he could 'read' the signatures of the toolmarks and if possible match them to each other. He was able to state confidently that three of the piles had been cut using one axe, two had been cut with another and the last did not match any. The work was part of his final year dissertation and he went on to develop the study as a PhD at the University of Edinburgh. He was able to match many of the piles from the site and even tie in some of the cut woodchips that are also found throughout the organic material (Sands 1997). This work was important as it allowed timbers that were not actually associated with each other to be assigned to the same period of construction.

However, this is an over-simplified description of Sands' work as he went on to examine the sorts of tools that were used, how they were used and the felling processes involved in acquiring the timbers to build the site. Possibly his most useful contribution after the importance of signature matching was his recognition of the importance of combining signature analysis with dendrochronology and the support that each method can give to the other (Sands 1997).

DENDROCHRONOLOGY

The wealth of timbers on Oakbank Crannog should be a useful reservoir of material for dendrochronological studies, however, there are problems. The first problem is that there is not yet a master chronology for Scotland. There is no continuous sequence of dates from the present projecting progressively further into the past into which Oakbank timbers might fit to give an absolute date. A number of oak samples were taken from Oakbank Crannog by Dr M. Baillie of Queen's University, Belfast in the hope that they might correlate with master chronologies for Ireland but unfortunately they did not match, probably because of climatic differences in the two areas.

A more useful area in which dendrochronology could contribute to our understanding of Oakbank is in the creation of a relative chronology of different phases of habitation and construction on the site. Positive results in this area of tree-ring studies have been achieved from Neolithic Continental lake-dwellings and from the prehistoric trackways of the Somerset Levels. Archaeologically different phases of building and repair are obvious at Oakbank but it is not always clear by visual observation which timbers relate to which chronological phases. The fact that distinct features and groups of piles are so readily discernible would seem to make this a case where site-specific dendrochronology would prove useful.

During the 1982 and 1983 seasons of work at Oakbank a large number of samples (> 250) were taken from timbers of all sorts, mostly alder, hazel and oak. The samples represented structural elements of the site and were examined by A. Crone at Sheffield University as one of two case studies for a PhD thesis (Crone 1988). Crone's work proved useful in supporting the idea of groups of timbers being cut down together and the same groups being used in distinct features on the site. However, she had to concentrate on alder timbers as they predominate on the site and there are few useful oaks, the preferred species for tree-ring analysis. Alder trees are very susceptible to poor weather and can stop growing for up to as much as five years making it very difficult to match them. Another problem with the Oakbank alder is that most of the trees are less than 40 years old which means there are too few rings to create long sequences of patterns for matching. The outcome is that Crone's work showed a number of 'blocks' of timbers that seem to have been felled at the same time and most of these can be matched visually on the site plans making useful corroboration although the groups of matching timbers are relatively small and in some cases they are inconclusive. However, there is great promise in the combination of her work with the signature matching developed by Sands and it is hopeful that in the future a research project can bring the two studies together and produce useful results for examining the details of the construction sequence.

SECTION B3–B4

In an effort to better understand the relationship between linear and vertical structural features, a 5m-wide section was cut through the site between control points B3 and B4 *(50, 51)*. The aim was to examine the foundation deposits and the relationship between the peripheral boulders and the many uprights around the edge of the site.

50 Section through Oakbank Crannog showing different phases of construction. *N. Dixon*

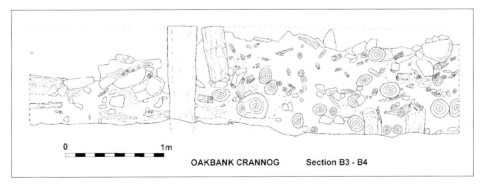

51 Drawing of section B3-B4.

Stratigraphy

Another reason for cutting the section was to see if it was possible to identify distinct stratigraphy within the organic deposit. It was already established that there were differences in texture and that in places layers could be clearly peeled off exposing deposits, obviously in situ, of insect puparia, animal droppings or seeds.

Clearly stratified deposits were observed in the section. The most obvious layering was seen in the east half of the section separate from the area of horizontal radial timbers. This may have been the result of differential disturbance. The material in the area where most construction and reconstruction took place would be periodically disturbed and mixed while the area with few timbers, and therefore with no building or rebuilding, would be relatively undisturbed.

Timber phasing

It was hoped that it would be possible to examine timbers in the section to see if they had been inserted at different times, thereby representing different phases of occupation. In the section, uprights were recorded that are primary piles since they are solidly driven into the loch-bed silts far enough to completely cover the cut points. They should represent the earliest phase of construction on the site. In contrast, other piles are clearly secondary uprights from a later phase of rebuilding, as the cut points have been driven into the organic deposit after the deposit had been laid to a depth of at least 90cm and possibly deeper. They do not penetrate through the organic deposit and into the loch bed. They may have been used to strengthen or replace the earlier piles.

The elevation also shows the cross-sections of a substantial number of longitudinal tree trunks restricted to the west half of the section. It is notable that the great majority of these timbers lie more or less radially in relation to the crannog and are found mostly in the lower half of the section. It is assumed that most of these are not still in situ though they may not be far from their original position and alignment. These timbers were transverse supports jointed to the numerous uprights nearby to carry the circumferential beams forming the walkway around the crannog. Presuming that the walkway was above water then the radial supports must also have been either above water or close to the surface. Therefore, when the connecting joints degraded the transverse timbers dropped and came to rest on the organic deposit building up on the loch bed. If this is the case the higher timbers may represent periods of structural repair and the replacement of rotted supports.

Compaction

It was also a matter of interest to observe by how much the loch bed silts had been compressed by the weight of the crannog material since this was conjectured as one of the reasons for the eventual submergence of this and other sites. In fact, it was considered by Robert Munro to be probably the major process of submergence.

The base of the mound lies flat on the loch bed with no evidence of a depression in the silt. The cause of submergence of Oakbank Crannog, and of the other submerged crannogs in Loch Tay, may be considered in terms of internal collapse and compaction as a result of biological and mechanical degradation and not by subsidence into soft loch-bed silts. The collapse was followed by an average rise in the loch level sometime after abandonment of the site and clearly seen in the old drowned shoreline around many parts of the loch.

Silting

The amount of silting that had taken place in the last two-and-a-half millennia was answered by examining the section. A substantial build-up could mean the preservation within the silts of the remains of canoes, fish-traps and objects which had fallen from the crannog when it was inhabited, as well as early foundation elements not protected by being embedded in the organic matrix.

The section demonstrated that in this part of the site there has been effectively no build-up of silt since construction of the crannog. The boulders and organic deposit lie on the original loch-bed silts and show no evidence of having been covered around the edges by later material. This may be partly a result of increased wave action in the shallow water. On the deep side of the site, silting had taken place as the tops of oak timbers were discovered under about half a metre of silt.

Construction technique

Another objective of cutting the section was to see whether the method of building crannogs, as put forward by Robert Munro, applied at Oakbank.

Munro said that a crannog was made by a timber raft that was floated out then sunk with stones, brushwood, peat and earth and held in position with piles driven through the material. There is no evidence in the section of any of these construction elements. Indeed, there is a significant lack of large stones within the organic matrix and particularly in association with the lower parts of uprights where they penetrate either the loch bed or the organic matrix and where they might be expected if Munro were correct. In fact, the evidence from Oakbank strongly suggests that the first structure on the site was a free-standing pile structure with open water under the platform that allowed the build-up of the stratified layers noted in the section.

The excavation of the section was proved justifiable by the information it supplied regarding the structure of the site and the formation of the remains in this area. It also showed that sections could be created and recorded and that their maintenance offered no significant problems underwater. The observations with respect to silting are of interest to this site and the discovery that no loch-bed subsidence has taken place is important for the contribution it makes to the general discussion of crannog submergence.

Twelve

SMALL FINDS AND ENVIRONMENTAL MATERIAL FROM OAKBANK CRANNOG

ARTEFACTS

Many exciting finds have come from the excavations over the years, including everyday domestic utensils, wooden and stone objects, wood chips and the waste from carpentry and slag from metalworking. There is also limited evidence of pottery and the occasional, sometimes surprising, flint such as an Early Bronze Age barbed and tanged arrowhead presumably picked up by the Iron Age crannog-dwellers. The largest group of finds is environmental material such as macro-plant remains, pollen, excreta and insects. The range of finds is wide and some of the evidence has never been seen before on prehistoric archaeological sites in Scotland. At Oakbank, all objects not natural to the site are classed as finds. Artefacts are objects made and modified by the human hand and include the residues of manufacture such as wood chips with cut marks on them. Other finds are natural objects brought into the crannog for one reason or another, such as the mass of plant remains.

The crannog at Oakbank is an almost wholly anthropogenic feature with minimal quantities of naturally deposited material. In a way, it can be regarded as a single, highly complex, artefact. Almost everything within, and including, the structure of the crannog is there by virtue of man's direct activities. This means that even a featureless stone on the site is there as a result of a purposeful act. The purpose may never be known, but its existence should be considered.

On a dry-land site it is often a relatively simple task to decide what is and what is not a find. Therefore, the decision of what to keep and what to discard is usually clear-cut. On a site like Oakbank the great majority of the material would be classed as finds in terms of dry-land excavation and the decision of what to keep and what to reject is by no means always obvious. For instance, there are probably millions of splinters or fragments of wood throughout the site. To discard all pieces which have no sign of working may be to discard a great deal of evidence for the construction of hurdles or the practice of coppicing. Many pieces are simply sharpened at the end but examination of them may reveal the tools used. To keep every piece with a cut end, however, may result in a massive collection of meaningless fragments of wood. Total quantitative analysis of such fragments would mean preserving the material from the whole crannog mound, an organic deposit of about 1,000 cu m.

In practice, the excavation of a site such as this must be seen as a sampling exercise. All timbers over about 10cm in diameter have a slice removed for examination, and in the case of larger pieces for dendrochronological analysis; unless there is tool mark evidence the rest of the timber is discarded. Although a representative collection of unworked pieces may be useful ultimately, there are no resources available for the very expensive conservation of such material.

The situation is the same with stones. Unless a stone shows positive evidence of having been used as a hammer, rubber or other tool, even though it comes from the habitation layer, it is not recovered. However, the stone dumps on the loch bed are not likely to be disturbed and would be available for analysis later if required.

The preservation on submerged sites is so good that many details of the way of life of the inhabitants can be clearly established. At Oakbank Crannog there is pottery with burnt food still sticking to the inside, remains of the only pot discovered so far. It is clear that the inhabitants relied heavily upon wood to make their domestic utensils which is hardly surprising in such a richly wooded area. Wooden plates and dishes, remains of a wooden cup for drinking, a wooden spoon, and a butter dish with remains of butter still sticking to the inside, have all been recovered. Agricultural practice is indicated by the discovery of a unique cultivation implement and a fragment of fine textile not suspected from this early date in Scotland shows a sophisticated taste in clothing. The cloth may have been traded into the area but if it was made on site, as suggested from the discovery of spindle whorls and the presence of sheep remains, then it shows a high level of skill in weaving.

Wooden artefacts

The majority of artefacts from the excavation so far are made of wood and they indicate a range of articles which also must have been commonplace on

52 Wooden plate after raising, showing loss of colour with exposure. *N. Dixon*

contemporary dry-land sites. They would have been as appropriate to the inhabitants of any type of site and are important for the insight they give into the range of domestic, craft and industrial equipment used in prehistoric households. Some of these artefacts are reported below.

Fine plate
A small round, finely cut, plate was discovered made of alder that shows a high level of woodworking skill *(38, 52)*. It is 18cm in diameter and the rim is 3cm high. The base is less than 5mm thick and is of an even thickness all over which shows a great deal of care in manufacture since it is not turned on a lathe. The rim is of a sloping triangular section with a strong but aesthetically pleasing appearance. Vertical tool-marks round the outside edge suggest the use of a gouge for final shaping. It was found two-thirds complete in four main pieces embedded in the organic matrix. The missing part was not found and the plate must have been damaged in antiquity and may have been discarded for this reason.

Coarse plate
In contrast to this finely cut plate was a coarse dish also made of alder *(53)*. It is very thick-sided and was hollowed out with little apparent effort made to smooth the surface of the wood. It appears to have been cut from a block of wood some

35cm long, 10cm wide and 10cm high. The upper edge is 2cm thick and the sides slope down into the interior so that they are progressively thicker towards the base. One long side and part of the base are missing and seem to have been eroded away after the rest of the dish became embedded in the organic matrix. While the round plate is best suited for humans to eat from, the coarse dish could have served a variety of purposes. It may have been a serving dish or a container for food, a small trough for animals or even a bailer for a canoe.

Large bowl

A much larger, oval-shaped wooden bowl was discovered which had an oak pile driven through the bottom, breaking it into four large pieces *(colour plate 20)*. This is not only good evidence of the sort of vessels owned by the crannog people but also shows clearly that the site was used, abandoned and rebuilt for later use. The bowl must have been deposited in an abandoned area of the site, just near the front entrance, where it was covered up with layers of bracken and other debris. Sometime later a number of large piles were driven into this area possibly to strengthen or rebuild the north-east corner of the platform. The builders driving the heavy oak pile would have felt little resistance as it penetrated the bowl. This is the area where the large threshold timber was also discovered adding to the idea of significant collapse having taken place here. The bowl was about 50cm by 35cm and may have been used for collecting and carrying fruit of some sort.

Drinking vessel

Another domestic find was a stave for a small container, which was probably made of apple or pear wood *(54)*. It is 6cm wide at the base and 12cm high. The bottom

53 Opposite Coarse wooden dish from Oakbank. *N. Dixon*

54 Right Stave from wooden cup. Circular base would fit into rebate around bottom. *N. Dixon*

0   **5 cm**

of the side wall is 1cm thick and it tapers to the rim. The bottom is rebated and the piece would have been one of six staves that would slot into a circular base to form a wooden cup. Resin might have been used to seal the joints and faint impressions on the outside may be evidence of binding with cord or leather. Its capacity is about 0.75l (1.5 pints) for liquid, but it could also have been a measure, possibly for grain or flour. Like the plate this object suggests substantial woodworking skill. The rebate is neatly cut and the taper from base to rim again points to an aesthetic consideration as opposed to the purely functional. The accuracy of constructing six pieces which fitted closely enough together to make the body of the vessel reasonably tight suggests the hand of an experienced woodworker.

Butter dish

The most exciting object in the domestic range were the remains of a rect-angular-shaped wooden dish which still had the remains of butter sticking to the inside *(colour plate 21)*. The dish was cut with a small tool and the marks are very clear over most of the the the surface. There were four holes about 2cm in diameter in the bottom of the dish and it is thought that these were to enable the milk product to drain from the butter during manufacture, however it is also possible that the vessel was used in cheese-making. This find alone adds significantly to our understanding of the animal husbandry of the crannog people as it obviously points to dairy produce as an important part of the diet.

Spindle whorl

The spinning of wool is indicated on the site by the discovery of a wooden spindle-whorl 5cm in diameter *(55)*. It was cut to shape, not turned on a lathe, and as with the other wooden artefacts the toolmarks were still fresh. The perforation was squared at one end and presumably the spindle was so shaped that it neither turned in the hole or fell out in use. The wooden spindle whorl is very light and may have been for spinning very fine fibres, such as nettle, while a heavier stone spindle whorl would have been more suitable for spinning wool.

55 Alder spindle whorl.
N. Dixon

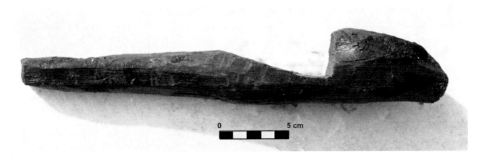

56 Alder peg. N. *Dixon*

Peg

The surface of a wooden peg 25cm long made of alder, admirably demonstrated the use of a sharp knife, about the size of a modern pen knife *(56)*. Similar tool-marks are also evident on most of the other small wooden finds. The original function of the peg is not known but the pronounced notch on one side points to a use where pressure is being taken in one direction. It would not, for instance, be used to tether an animal which could pull in all directions, but could take the strain on a rope used for holding down a haystack or a roof covering.

Paddles

A wooden paddle made of alder, 1.35cm long, was similar in form to modern canoe paddles with a convex back to the blade and a relatively flat face *(57)*. A notch in the edge of the blade near the handle may be where it rubbed against the side of a canoe suggesting that it might have been used as a steering oar rather than as a paddle. Toolmarks are clearly visible on the blade. Significantly, another paddle was found recently near the same area and it is quite different in form *(58)*. It looks more like the sort of paddle that would be used to power a logboat. It is possible that the two discoveries are the steering oar and the paddle for power of a logboat belonging to the crannog-dwellers. Although no logboat has so far been found at Oakbank Crannog, a large oak logboat 11.5 m long, dating to the Bronze Age, was discovered at the crannog reconstruction near Kenmore. Logboats were often found near crannogs examined in the past and were almost certainly in use at Oakbank. It is assumed that the finds are paddles for a boat of some sort but it has been shown that similar implements were, and still are, used for winnowing grain (Lerche and Steensberg 1971, 87-104). High concentrations of cereal pollen from the site point to the cultivation of crops but the use of canoes is also a certainty.

57 Oar-shaped canoe paddle made of alder. N. Dixon

0   15 cm

58 Canoe paddle made of alder. N. Dixon

Cultivation implement

A find of considerable significance for evidence of arable cultivation by the crannog-dwellers was that of a complete oak implement for cultivation *(59)*. It was found at a level corresponding to that of the lower floor-foundation timbers and it has been suggested that such tools were deposited under floors as votive offerings. The Oakbank implement looks like a crook ard, or primitive horse-drawn plough, but it does not operate in the same way. It is a one-piece implement and could best be used like the Hebridean cas-chrom or foot plough. The direction of operation of the ard is indicated by a well-formed tang for digging into the soil, and a notch out of the wood may suggest that originally there had been a metal share attached to it.

The Oakbank ard is an important find and it aptly demonstrates a number of important aspects of well-preserved finds from crannogs. In practical terms it shows the care taken to use a strong type of wood, to utilise the natural formation of the branches and to take full advantage of the attributes of different parts of the wood. It is evidence of the form of cultivation carried out and by association indicates, to some degree, the economic and social structure of the society. It also

59 Cultivation implement made of oak. *N. Dixon*

further extends the range of prehistoric cultivation implements found in Scotland and shows a greater diversity of type than has so far been seen.

Whistle
An evocative find is a small whistle just over 5cm long made of dogrose or cherry *(colour plate 22)*. It may have been functional for attracting the attention of people or animals, perhaps a dog. Alternatively it may just have been a toy made by, or for, the crannog children.

Other wooden objects
Other finds of wooden objects are tantalisingly functional in their appearance but are so fragmentary as to be beyond recognition. A substantial, apparently dressed, piece of oak with an arc cut from one edge looks like part of a yoke for draft animals. A number of pieces of basketwork have emerged but all are fragmentary and do not indicate their original purpose. There are also a number of twisted hazel objects some of which are the remains of broken hurdles *(60, colour plate 23)*. It is not possible to say what others, in the shape of complicated knots, were used for but they were clearly manufactured for specific purposes.

Nineteen wooden pins have been discovered during excavation, of which sixteen were hazel, two were hazel or alder and one was oak. Most are 5-15cm long and 1-3cm in diameter. They displayed various degrees of cutting ranging between those with one simple angled cut to sharpen the end and those where facets cover the piece of wood and both ends are worked.

60 Hazel knot in organic matrix. *B.L. Andrian*

None were found in a position which might have indicated their original function but the possibilities are many. Leatherworkers would use such points for staking out skins during scraping. They could be used in weaving to fasten parts of the loom or the threads to the loom. They could be used for holding the hasp on a door or for holding hurdles or thatching in place. They would be used in rope making or for tightening loose joints in wooden structures. It is possible that future excavation may recover examples in situ.

TYPES OF WOOD

The crannog-dwellers have shown considerable capability in woodworking. It is also evident that they considered the properties of different types of wood for specific jobs. Hazel was specifically selected for the manufacture of many of the wooden points and other types of wood were also used for specific purposes. About 50 splinters of roughly split wood exhibited evidence of having been burnt at one end. They were from 3-10cm long and had the appearance of tapers which is how they are construed. All except one, which was alder, were cut from pine, a resinous wood which burns well when dry. The resin would keep the taper burning even with a small flame. It is notable that in the list of more than 370 wood species' identifications from the site, apart from the tapers, only one waste wood chip was pine.

Of the many structural uprights which have been examined, the great majority were alder, the next most common is oak and there are a number of large elms. Rowan, hazel and willow piles were also found but in very small numbers as they are not usually big or strong enough to support major structural elements. The importance of specific types of wood for specific tasks is clear.

TEXTILE

A small remnant of handspun woollen textile *(61)* was discovered at Oakbank Crannog. Examination concluded it was woven in a 2:1 twill which is a very fine and strong type of cloth, sometimes still used to make kilts (Heckett 1990). A dye test was also carried out on the cloth but proved negative. Discoveries of prehistoric cloth in Scotland are rare; prior to the excavation at Oakbank the earliest dated cloth was attributed to the thirteenth century AD.

STONE ARTEFACTS

Of the substantial number of stones from the site few showed conclusive proof of having carried out a specific function *(colour plate 24)*. A group of roughly perforated stones 10-15cm in diameter may have been used as net or loom weights. They are

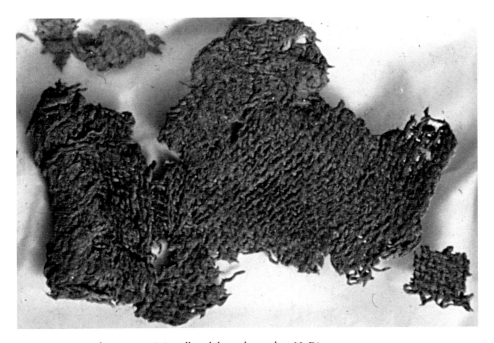

61 Fragment textile woven in 2:1 twill with hem along edge. *N. Dixon*

sub-circular with apparently little attempt made to shape them accurately and the only feature to show that they were functional is the hole in the middle. A smaller, but otherwise similar, stone 8cm in diameter may have been too light to have been a loom weight but along with an even smaller and smoother perforated stone 4cm in diameter it could have been a spindle whorl used for drop-spinning wool by hand.

The abundant tool marks on timbers throughout the site point to cutting with a range of sharp metal tools. A number of stones have been smoothed or flattened and may have been used as whetstones, though only one shows clear ridging where thin blades or points were sharpened. A large stone 40cm x 18cm is dipped in the middle and was used as a quern for grinding grain while other stones of various sizes could well have been used as hammers or rubbers but do not have conclusive wear patterns. A sandstone cup about 10cm in diameter was also found.

The most accomplished piece of stonework is a stone bead 13mm in diameter with a neat hour-glass perforation not quite in the centre. It is probably from a necklace or bracelet and it is polished smooth. One jet bead or ring was found 25mm in diameter with a large straight-sided perforation through the centre. Marks of working can be seen in a few regular striations around the edge. Another decorative object was a small sandstone pendant *(62)* with a hole through one end. It would have hung around the neck possibly on a leather thong. These three objects make it clear that the inhabitants of the crannog had reason to care about ornamental belongings and, if they

62 Sandstone pendant. *N. Dixon*

63 Pottery with burnt food stuck to inside. *N. Dixon*

manufactured the objects on site, that they were as delicate in working stone as they could be with wood. If these were manufactured elsewhere it would be very interesting to learn of the exchange mechanism by which they arrived on the crannog. The jet bead is almost certainly an import as finds of jet from this period come mainly from the north-east of England.

POTTERY

Remains of few pottery vessels have been discovered, presumably owing to the abundance of wood in the area and the relative scarcity of good clay. Some vessels are represented by single small sherds but one vessel had hundreds of fragments and some substantial sherds *(63)*. They may be the complete remains of the pot since they were all found in close association and the two largest pieces are joinable. The fabric of the pot was very coarse and there was crude decoration in the form of a string impression. The fabric included very large quartz grits and the form was simple. Outside the clay is grey-pink but it is black on the inside.

One of the most informative features of the pot was observed when the pieces were allowed to dry. A black charcoaly deposit had been noted adhering to the inside of the vessel. On drying it began to shrink and crack. In some cases the black deposit was about 1cm thick and upon analysis it was proved by amino acid content to be the remains of food. Due to the high level of carbonisation, it was not possible to distinguish whether the food was meat or vegetable. The deposit was so thick and so carbonised that it may well have resulted in the pot being thrown out. The remains were lying on top of the organic deposit underneath the upper stones and must relate to a late phase of occupation just before the stones were deposited. It is also in a position that would have been just outside the front door and it is easy to imagine the flaming pot being thrown out before it set the house on fire.

METALWORK

A number of metal objects have been found on the site. One of the most interesting is a small iron knife *(64)*. It is one of the key artefacts that puts the site firmly in the Iron Age as the early radiocarbon dates indicated that the crannog could be either Late Bronze Age or Early Iron Age. The toolmarks on timbers of all sizes point to the use of a good range of tools and this is supported by the work of a student at Edinburgh University (Sands 1997). The knife had a tang at one end and it may have been used in the manufacture of the smaller wooden objects including the pegs and the butter dish with their very clear tool-marks.

The only diagnostic find from the site so far is a swan's neck pin *(65)* which was discovered in 2002. It is a type more commonly seen further south and on the Continent although the Oakbank example is slightly different in form. According to Professor Dennis Harding of Edinburgh University:

> It is an intermediate between a swan's neck pin (sometimes derived from the disc-headed swan's neck pins of the Late Bronze Age), and a crook-headed pin, which is one Scottish variant of the ring-headed pins that generally succeeded swan's neck pins. (*Harding pers comm.*)

The pin can be seen as a prestige object and was almost certainly traded into the area. It is another clear indicator of the relatively high status of these crannog-dwellers.

A number of pieces of slag have also been excavated suggesting that metalworking was being carried out on the site. It is unlikely to have been iron-working given the high temperatures and sophisticated furnaces and hearths required for that, but small-scale bronze working would have been possible and the discovery of a fragment of a small crucible supports the idea.

BONE

Other finds included scatters of burnt bone fragments in all parts of the site. The individual fragments were not large enough to be diagnostic. Unburnt bone, although in a relatively poor state of preservation was easily recognisable as, most

64 Small iron knife. *N. Dixon*

65 Swan's neck pin typically dated to transition between Bronze and Iron Ages. *N. Dixon*

commonly, fragments of the jaw-bones and teeth *(66)* of cattle and other animals. The teeth were in a better state of preservation than the bone though the cusps in the centre of the tooth structure often fell out as the soft material around them had deteriorated. So far the majority of teeth are those of cattle of various ages, with smaller numbers of sheep, goat and pig. Wear on the pig teeth indicated both young and mature beasts.

The finds from Oakbank Crannog give a clear picture of aspects of the way of life led by the crannog-dwellers but there are some interesting omissions from the evidence so far. It is notable that no bones of wild animals have been

66 Jawbone of sheep. *N. Dixon*

recognised and there is no evidence of fishing. Throughout history, Loch Tay has been important for both fishing and hunting and that is still the case today; yet the people of the crannog did not seem to involve themselves in these lucrative pastimes which would surely have broadened their diet. It is possible, given that there is so much evidence for agriculture, that the people were concentrating on farming and did not see it necessary to go out hunting and fishing. After all, they could always exchange some beef, pork or lamb for salmon or venison if they felt the need. It may be that we are seeing a level of the developed hierarchy in the area with wealthy farmers living on their crannog, fishermen living around the shores and hunters in the woods and on the hills above the loch where they would find their game. It will be interesting to see if the same distribution of food types is found when other crannogs in the loch are sampled.

ENVIRONMENTAL EVIDENCE

The bare, barren mountains around the loch immediately after the glaciers left 10,000 years ago have, for the most part, been clothed in thick deciduous woodlands which would have been home to wild animals of all sorts including, bear, wolf and wild boar. In and around the woods and on the higher slopes of the mountains grew a wide variety of plant types that were an important source of food for the people who inhabited the area. Many of these plants are now considered no more than weeds but underwater excavation clearly demonstrates their common use in the past and our ancestors would have been familiar with them not so long ago. A resurgence of interest today is reflected in the wider availability and practice of herbal remedies and homeopathic treatments.

The largest group of finds from Oakbank Crannog falls, not surprisingly, under the heading of environmental material. Much of it helps to reconstruct the environment in which the crannog-dwellers lived but also the manner of their exploitation of that environment. The range of trees, shrubs, grasses and cereals found on the adjacent loch shores is displayed in the materials used to construct and reconstruct the different elements of the site, the flooring, insulation and bedding on which the inhabitants and their animals lived and the food which they ate. The types of animals are represented by well-preserved excreta. The excreta itself offered sustenance to insects and parasites which have been preserved in it and in the floor-covering on which it dropped. The remains of Oakbank Crannog consist of about 1,000 cu m of this material and analyses so far have proved very exciting and informative. The evidence from specialists who have examined material from the site can only be summarised here but their works are listed at the end.

Pollen analysis
The first substantial botanical study at Oakbank was pollen analysis carried out on a core taken through the site acquired in 1982 by driving a 10cm diameter plastic drainpipe from the top of the organic deposit down into the loch bed.

Examination of the core was carried out by Dr R. Scaife of the Department of the Environment based in the Institute of Archaeology, London (Clapham and Scaife 1988). The bottom 12cm of the core consisted of loch-bed sands mixed with spores and pollen and the rest of the column represented occupation of the site. Scaife recognised two floor construction levels from breaks in the layers of material and from the pollen types. The upper occupation layer contained substantial amounts of straw with wood at the top of the deposit and the lower layer contained greater amounts of wood throughout without any evidence of straw.

One of the most interesting observations made by Scaife was an unnaturally high proportion of spores to pollen at the base of the crannog mound. Most of the spores are ferns (*Dryopteris*) with lesser amounts of bracken (*Pteridium aquilinum*). This fits in well with the idea of the site as a free-standing structure in the early phases of occupation. If ferns and bracken were laid as flooring or bedding on a platform above water the spores and pollen from the material would fall through the gaps in the woodwork and build up on the loch bed. Over a period of time this would produce high concentrations until, eventually, the ends of the floor supports would rot and the floor with its overburden collapse onto the loch bed covering the area of concentrated spores. Later rebuilding would be on a mound, not a free-standing pile-dwelling, so the build-up of spores would be more evenly dispersed.

Another phase of early occupation at the site can be seen in the predominance of fern as opposed to bracken spores in the bottom layers. Ferns grow best in woodland where it is shaded but as the trees are cut down bracken will grow around the edges and become the dominant form. So ferns used in the early years would become less common and bracken would then become the main floor covering.

Tree types in the core are dominated by pollen of alder and hazel with evidence of oak and elm. Pine and birch are also represented. Scaife sees this as indicating the vegetation of the shore with alder round the edge of the loch, as it is today, and hazel on slightly drier ground. Alder/hazel domination of the arboreal pollen persisted throughout the period of occupation of the site.

It seems likely that even at this level hazel would have been exploited: foliage could be used as animal fodder and bedding; nuts as human food; and wood for artefacts and fencing. The percentage of hazel pollen throughout the site is likely to be distorted by anthropogenic factors, the great amount brought in by the crannog-dwellers for the many uses they had for hazel, and the macro-plant evidence shows this to be the case.

Seeds and macro-plant remains

The most comprehensive group of materials are the macro-plant remains including every part of the plant such as stalks and stems, leaves, twigs, roots, seeds and fruits. Although obvious plant remains are seen throughout Oakbank Crannog while excavating, the true wealth of the environmental record is best seen through the microscope in laboratory conditions.

Over the years a number of researchers have carried out analyses of samples from the site and have all made an important contribution to our understanding of the crannog people and their exploitation of their environment. The work has progressed from a few samples in polythene bags and flower pots, to a core through the depth of the site in a relatively shallow area to a sampling regime to answer specific questions. Sampling of all deposits goes on now as a natural part of the excavation although one of the greatest expenses in post-excavation is the cost of the laboratory work.

It is impossible to go into great detail about all of the plant remains from Oakbank Crannog and their possible uses. In working for her doctoral thesis Jennifer Miller of Glasgow University identified 166 different sorts of plant types from the site (Miller 1997, 2002). She is not the only person to have examined samples from

Oakbank but her research is the most comprehensive and was specifically related to the site as a settlement and to the functions carried out there. Her work focused on the macro-plant remains and she identified a number of plants not seen so early in Scotland (Miller *et al* 1998).

AGRICULTURE AT THE CRANNOG

There is very strong evidence that crannog-dwellers were farmers and that agriculture played a major part in their lives. Some of the artefacts have shown the different aspects of farming practised such as the cultivation implement suggesting arable farming; the butter dish with its evidence of dairying; the animal bones of cattle, sheep or goats, and pigs showing the importance of animal husbandry and spindle whorls and spindles that indicate the presence of sheep exploited for wool. The plant remains supported the dominant part farming played in life on the crannog.

Cereals

The main cereal crops discovered at Oakbank were barley (*Hordeum vulgare*) and two sorts of wheat, emmer (*Triticum dicoccum*) and spelt (*Triticum spelta*).

Emmer and spelt wheat are genetically different types and emmer was the most common from the Neolithic period. They are both found in abundance at Oakbank and both yield high protein flour. Spelt is more resistant to cold, wind and disease and is therefore better suited to the climate around Loch Tay, particularly with the onset of the Iron Age and a poorer climate than existed in the Neolithic and Bronze Ages.

Barley is more common on the crannog and it has been the staple grain in the country for a very long time. Although it is nutritionally inferior to wheat it is hardier and more reliable and ripens in a shorter time meaning that it can be sown in the spring and harvested before the potentially bad autumn weather common in Scotland. Wheat is valued more highly than barley but is best sown in autumn. Together the two different types of grain mean the crannog-dwellers could spread the risk and have a better chance of a good yield.

Another difference between the two grains is that wheat is easier to process as barley needs more threshing. Barley is also the most popular food supplement for animals and there is good evidence from the Oakbank samples that it was used for this purpose. It is also well known for its use in brewing beer although no evidence for that has been found yet at the crannog.

Miller identified three different areas where cereal was discovered on the site and each area suggested a specific utilisation of the remains. Just outside the front door of the crannog, in areas A2 and A3, the samples indicated cereal levels that suggested processing the grain in this area. This would have been the final sieving and fine cleaning of the grain which in the case of wheat would have been a meticulous task because of its high value. Many weed seeds were found in the samples typical of types that are common in grain and would have been harvested with it. Evidence of flax and wild-fruit processing was also found in this area and it is the logical place to carry out such processing without transporting it all around the house.

On and around the living floors of the house, in areas B4, C2 and C6, the combinations of grain refuse, including chaff, tail grain and some good grain suggest its use as fodder for the animals that would be housed on the crannog. Elsewhere throughout the house there was a general scatter of all parts of the plants which shows a general presence but no specific purpose. Clearly where there are concentrations of specific types of grain and particular parts of the plant they are indicative of areas with a specific function.

The spelt wheat from Oakbank Crannog is the earliest occurrence of this grain in Scotland by 500 years and much earlier than had been supposed. It shows the farming skill of the people and their clear understanding of different types of grain and the benefits of each. Spelt wheat would be particularly good for bread while emmer wheat made good porridge.

Other nutritious plants

Vegetables as we know them date back only as far as the Medieval period, long after the occupation of Oakbank Crannog . However, wild species from the same families were found at Oakbank. These plants would not be recognised on the shelves in the supermarket today but wild species of cabbage and turnip (*brassica species*), wild carrots (*daucus*), and hedge mustard (*sisymbrium officinale*) were on the site along with species such as Fat Hen (*chenopodium album*) which is an excellent source of iron and one of the most important green leafy plants of the past found on many archaeological sites. These plants would have grown naturally on waste ground, in clearings and around the margins of arable fields, and leaves, shoots and tubers would have been collected as nutritious foodstuffs to supplement the staple diet.

Many plants are indicative of human activity in terms of land disturbance but are also plants with food value. Many are weeds associated with land disturbance such as forest clearance, and particularly with the practice of arable cultivation, and include things like nettles (*urticaceae*) which we now consider pests. The people in the past recognised that nettles can be used for fibre to produce very fine cloth. The leaves are also a good addition to stews and are a good source of iron. Nipplewort (*lapsana communis*) was well represented at Oakbank and has been found in archaeological contexts since Neolithic times (Renfrew 1973, 173). Knotgrass (*polygonaceae*) has also been recorded from archaeological sites where it seems to have been deliberately collected in the Early Iron Age. It is commonly found with cereals and, as a source of food, may have been processed into flour (Renfrew 1973, 182).

Other plants would undoubtedly have been eaten too, although evidence for them was not recovered. According to Miller:

> A likely additional supplement to the diet would have been the underground storage stems of silverweed (*potentilla anserina*). Silverweed grows around the Loch today and the swollen stems have a delicate nutty flavour. Seeds of Potentilla are difficult to differentiate, other than a few species, and it may be that silverweed was found at Oakbank, but not recognised as such. In any case, the plant would have been dug up off site and the underground stems brought back, indicating that seeds might not ever have been prolific on the site. (*Miller pers comm.*)

It should be remembered that even with the contributions of a number of researchers, including Miller's substantial work, the samples that have been examined from Oakbank so far are only a fraction of the material comprising the whole site.

Fruits and nuts at Oakbank Crannog
In all parts of the site seeds and fruits, or parts of them, are discovered and can easily be recognised by even the botanically untrained observer *(67)*. Individual examples are scattered everywhere but occasionally a group in close association is uncovered. The most obvious type, because of their size and ubiquity, are the broken shells of hazelnuts and occasionally the whole nut. On a number of crannog sites in Loch Tay, and elsewhere, hazelnut shells were observed around the base or on the flat top of the mound associated usually with evidence of other organic remains in the form of timbers or plant debris. This supports the evidence of many references to hazelnut shells being found in substantial quantities on submerged archaeological sites and presumably used as food since they are almost always broken. They were exploited as far back as the Mesolithic period and were ubiquitous on the Swiss lakeside sites, while as long ago as 1882 Munro commented, 'In all the lake-dwellings that have come under my own observation, the broken shells of hazelnuts were in profuse abundance' (1882, 283).

We take for granted the range of sweets and fruits available to us now but in the past the choice was much more restricted with wild fruits and honey the main sources of sweet food. The prehistoric people of Loch Tay exploited the woodlands and hillsides around them to collect a range of berries.

Stones of sloes and less commonly bird cherry, are almost as abundant as hazelnuts on the site but since the fruit of the cherry is on the outside the stones are left

67 Hazelnuts and an acorn. *N. Dixon*

complete. They were eaten as food by the humans, although bird cherries contain cyanide and neither of them is particularly sweet, but since the stones are not fragmented it would seem unlikely that they were fed to the animals.

It is notable that cherry (*prunus*) is not heavily represented in the pollen record although there are many stones of the fruit among the macro-plant remains. This may indicate that the foliage was not used as bedding or flooring and that it was not fed to the animals. It is also not represented on the site among the species exploited for their wood, with the possible exception of the whistle which may be cherry or dogrose. Although cherry trees are today found on the loch shore directly adjacent to the site, in antiquity they may not have been in such close proximity and may have required collecting from a distance if they were valued for food. This could also explain their absence from the pollen record but it is more likely that they were deliberately protected as a valued source of fruit.

Raspberries and brambles were also gathered by the crannog-dwellers and it seems likely that they would have gone to some effort to look after the bushes to ensure a good supply. They would have grown readily in the disturbed ground around the crannog fields and throughout the summer would have been a good source of vitamins. Wild strawberries and bilberries, or blaeberries as they are known in Scotland, were also found but not in such abundance as raspberries. This is probably because they are both very small types of berry and are often eaten straight from the plant as it would take a lot of collecting to gather sufficient to make it worthwhile taking them home.

A particularly exciting find was the discovery of five seeds of cloudberry. This plant only grows above 700m and the crannog people must have made special efforts to collect them, unless they were brought back with the flocks which were taken to higher pastures. Cloudberries are a delicacy and relatively common in Scandinavia but they are hard to find now in Scotland. They are known of in the Lawers range of mountains near to the site but are not common even there. They like acidic conditions and are found mainly associated with marsh and peat bogs. Their occurrence at Oakbank may hint at the practice of transhumance as stock were taken to upper pastures in the summer with the opportunity to collect cloudberries.

Other useful plants

Cultivated flax (*linum ussitatissimum*) was represented in both the seed sample and the pollen record at Oakbank and is a commonly recognised cereal of importance from as early as the fifth millennium BC in the Near East and at Neolithic Windmill Hill in Britain (Renfrew 1973, 120). It is valuable as a source of oil and fibre but was probably most valued for oil at Oakbank. The development and uses of flax are well covered elsewhere and its importance is only noted here.

INSECTS

Insect remains were recorded during the excavation of Oakbank Crannog. Parts of beetles, recognised as the dung beetle, were occasionally uncovered. They were readily recognisable as elytra, head, legs and mouth parts but many microscopic remains must also be present and have indeed been observed in the laboratory. The most common remains were the puparia of flies which were discovered in layers during excavation but were also recovered from organic samples. The action of other insects is indicated by tracks made on the sapwood of timbers beneath the bark *(68)*.

It is hardly surprising that samples have already yielded so much because of the wide range of eco-niches within the structure of the crannog. In the house there were functional areas for cooking, storing, food processing, weaving and spinning that all provided a range of habitats from small dark corners to holes in the thatch. The materials related to these niches would attract particular vermin. Outside the house was the open walkway, and also no doubt a midden area, plus

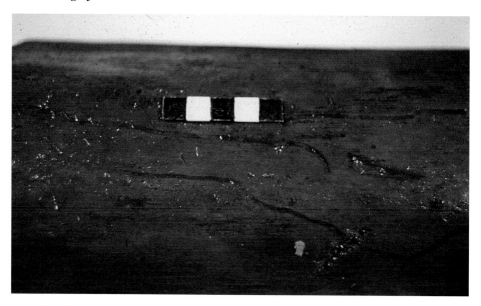

68 Marks of insect on sapwood beneath bark of tree. *N. Dixon*

the large extent of the water/crannog interface. The range of environments available would have been the homes of many creatures such as spiders, woodlice, snails, worms and insects including beetles, flies, wasps and earwigs. The potential is excellent for examining this wide range of creatures in such a complete state of preservation; in many instances they are still within the remains of their unique environment.

CONCLUSION

Pollen and macro-plant remains analysed from the crannog excavation show a landscape in which a wide variety of plant types was available for exploitation. The evidence showing how early societies used the landscape as a resource is contained in the mass of material excavated at Oakbank Crannog. It is clear that the crannog-dwellers roved far and wide to collect plants and seeds for consumption and for use around the house from the fruit and nuts and other food plants they gathered to the bracken and ferns they laid on the floor and used for bedding and insulation. There can be no doubt that the crannog-dwellers were extremely knowledgeable about the environment around them and were very skilful in its exploitation. Today we can learn a great deal about sustainable development from understanding the practices of our Early Iron Age ancestors.

Thirteen

INTERPRETATION

INTRODUCTION

One of the basic aims of archaeology is to reconstruct the past in as much detail as possible. This does not mean simply reconstructing objects and buildings; it also means interpreting the way of life led by people in the past and every aspect of that life and its place in the environment. The task is immense and many parts of it will never be explained as we can never know what people actually thought or felt. Archaeological excavation is an important method of acquiring data to understand the past. The better preserved the material remains, the greater the level of interpretation that can be attained through scientific analysis.

After considering the evidence from Oakbank Crannog for many years, we believed that the remains were sufficiently comprehensive to allow the recreation of a full-scale crannog in Loch Tay and that project started in 1994. The original site evidence did not show the outline and details of a complete crannog but there were enough clear features to enable a credible construction.

There were a number of reasons for building the crannog at Loch Tay, but they fall into three areas of particular interest: experimental archaeology and interpretation; education and raising awareness; and fund-raising to further research and training.

EXPERIMENTAL ARCHAEOLOGY AND INTERPRETATION

Elements of the project can be considered as experimental archaeology where the experimental aspects can assist in the interpretation of the original site. Of particular interest are the use of traditional materials and the way they stand up to the conditions in the loch, particularly to the weather which can be harsh in winter.

Many questions arose while excavating Oakbank Crannog relating to the structure and the methods that might have been used to construct it. We wanted to know how the crannog-builders drove the hundreds of piles, many of which were more than 7m long, into the loch bed. Initial experiments at Oakbank had been carried out by cutting down a small alder tree, cutting it to a point and attempting to drive it into the loch bed *(colour plate 27)*. A branch was cut in the shape of a large mallet but proved totally inappropriate for driving in even the small pile and some of those from the site were much bigger. Even hitting the pile with a large rock had no appreciable effect.

The method we used during the reconstruction was to cut the pile to a sharp point, pull it upright and wiggle it back and forth *(colour plate 28)*. The weight of the timber and the sharp point, combined with the momentum generated by twisting, effectively drove the pile into the loch bed to a depth of about 1.5m. While observing this happening under water we made another discovery. As the pile was driven into the loch bed, water was injected into the underlying clay making it malleable and allowing the pile to penetrate. White clay, displaced by the pile, was seen bubbling up around the point *(70)*. After a few hours the water came out of the clay and the pile was held firmly in the bottom. Once the clay was re-compacted the pile could not be moved sideways and could not be pushed deeper. The loch-bed clay is obviously a major feature in the strength of the overall crannog structure.

Leading from this discovery another subject became clearer. There were stones on the top of the original site, presumably to support upright timbers, but there were none around the original piles in the loch bed. Clearly, in the original construction the piles in the loch-bed clay did not need any extra support. However, in secondary phases of construction the piles were only driven into the artificially deposited organic mound and that did not offer the same support as the clay and so the piles had to be supported with stones. It would in any case be much easier to pile stones around the base of relatively shallow piles rather than those in deeper water.

While all of the details of the crannog reconstruction at the Scottish Crannog Centre do not match exactly the discoveries from Oakbank Crannog, the overall effect is intended to be as close to the original as possible *(colour plates 29, 30)*. Methods and materials which would have been available in the past were used where practicable. Much of the building work is clearly based on the results of archaeological research from a site where the species, size and condition of timbers is still readily observed. The floors and wall uprights in the reconstruction are true representations and many of the details of life on the crannog are very accurately portrayed. As work continues at Oakbank Crannog it is intended to incorporate new evidence into the reconstruction bringing it closer and closer to the condition of the original site.

70 White loch-bed clay bubbling up around newly driven pile. *B.L. Andrian*

Building the reconstruction taught us a great deal about what was required of the original crannog-builders (Dixon 2000). Many issues of the construction, the sourcing and harvesting of raw materials, the range of skilled and unskilled tasks performed and the size of workforce needed to perform them became clear. We have learned since that it is also important to observe the overall stability of the site and to examine the results of monitoring the different structural elements as time passes. In effect, the new crannog is a living experiment as we continue to learn from it both as a structure and as a home.

EDUCATIONAL RESOURCE

Another reason for building the reconstruction was to create a platform for teaching school children, university students and the general public about their heritage. We also hoped to encourage them to take an interest in history and archaeology, and specifically in underwater archaeology. Therefore, we explain the methods and techniques used to excavate Oakbank Crannog so that visitors know the background to underwater archaeology and how it contributes to our understanding of crannogs from the earliest times.

The people who lived on Oakbank Crannog in the Early Iron Age lived much of their lives on shore and ranged widely in the landscape around them. It is the aim of the Scottish Crannog Centre to involve visitors and researchers at all levels with the craft skills and associated activities that may have been an integral part of the way of life of the crannog-dwellers. Associated activities include fire-making, turning wood, rope-making, spinning and weaving, making holes in stones and hurdle-making.

In conjunction with the local Education Authorities an education pack was produced and distributed to all the schools in the Tayside area. It covered the underwater excavation and interpretation of Oakbank Crannog leading to the crannog reconstruction. New teaching materials are continually being developed today.

RAISE AWARENESS AND RAISE FUNDS

An important reason for setting up the Scottish Crannog Centre with the reconstruction at its heart was to fund the continuing excavations at Oakbank Crannog and to allow the other 17 sites in the loch, and the hundreds of others throughout Scotland, to be examined in more detail. A programme of public talks is carried out each year and an integral part of the Centre's work is to educate and enlighten everyone about the importance of Scotland's submerged cultural heritage and the importance of Underwater and Experimental Archaeology.

Construction of the full-sized crannog began in June 1994 and the site was officially opened to the public in July 1997; since then more than 150,000 visitors have experienced the past that has been recreated there. Funding remains an issue, however, as the Centre is an independent organisation that receives no fixed subsidies and so relies on admissions and donations to meet operating costs.

HOW THE RECONSTRUCTION WAS CONCEIVED

The recreated crannog was not born of a ready-made kit or concept; it developed gradually from other sorts of reconstruction that had been attempted over the years.

Paintings and drawings

The first artist's impression of Oakbank Crannog was produced in 1982 for the cover of a colour magazine, and the next was a painting for a television programme produced by the BBC in 1985 *(colour plate 25)*. These were adequate at first, but soon many aspects became archaeologically unacceptable as more excavation enabled greater interpretation of Oakbank Crannog. In particular, we determined that the original crannog was a free-standing pile-dwelling and stones would not, originally, have been evident around the base of the supporting piles. Also, the slope of the roof in early illustrations was too low. Practical considerations dictated a steeper pitch to the thatched roof to allow rain to run off rather than penetrate and rot the thatch, and to help snow to slip off before the weight of it could cause collapse.

Eventually, an isometric view of the crannog with part of the roof and walls cut away so the interior can be seen was drawn by Alan Braby, a talented archaeological illustrator in Scotland *(69)*. The scene is populated with the inhabitants of the site carrying out some of the everyday tasks that may have taken place. One man is building the fence around the outside of the platform while another cuts a point on large timbers for use as upright piles. Another man carries a coracle and others are bringing sheep onto the site. Another is sharpening his spear and a woman is talking to a young girl while a cauldron hangs over the fire. The site is divided into functional areas for living and working. While there is not evidence from Oakbank Crannog for every one of these activities the overall scene and construction are an accurate general representation of the site and activities that may well have been carried out

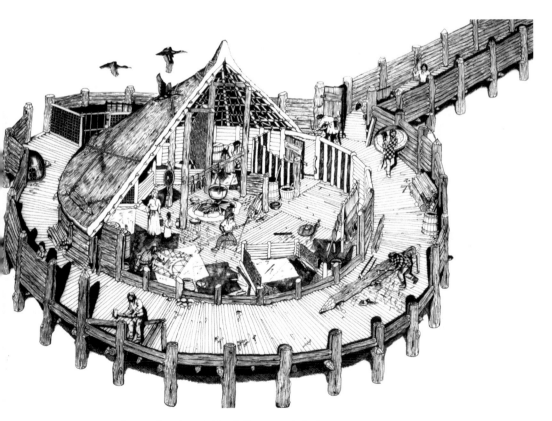

69 Reconstruction drawing based on Oakbank Crannog. *A. Braby*

there. There is certainly clear evidence for some of the activities, such as pointing the piles, building the fence, bringing in the sheep and for much of the structure, such as the floor of undressed logs laid side by side, the hurdle partition walls and the division of the house into discrete areas. Necessarily in such an image, there are still many features missing, such as how the beams that supported the floor would have been attached to the supporting piles.

Scale model

The almost inevitable next step from drawings and paintings of the site is the construction of a model *(colour plate 26)*. In the case of Oakbank Crannog, this was undertaken by a long-standing member of the STUA, David Jones, who produced it from the materials found in his garden and based it on Braby's drawings and discussions with the archaeologists. Once more, while there are obvious omissions, particularly in structural details, the main interpretative strength of the model lies in the overall impression it conveys.

Engineers' drawings and model

While the crannog model had a number of drawbacks it was sufficiently accurate to be shown to the planning authorities as an example of what was wanted in Loch Tay. However, impressed as they seemed to be the planners required more accurate and detailed engineers' drawings to ensure that the intended structure would stand up safely to the rigours of an educational visitor centre with, potentially, 25,000 visitors a year.

CONCLUSION

Underwater archaeology is a useful interpretative tool; it provides a method of gaining insight into the details of buildings and other structures at a level unknown on dry land sites. The preservation and analysis of organic materials that normally rot away very quickly on land not only enables us to reconstruct past environments, but also yields a wealth of evidence for the architectural elements of past communities and the detailed aspects of their entire life and interaction with those environments. This clear picture also allows experimental reconstruction at all levels and enables public observation and participation of aspects of life in the past in an educational and exciting way. It is hoped that in the future the way of life of past communities will become more understood by the public through the combination of underwater archaeology, experimental archaeology, public archaeology and cultural tourism.

Fourteen

SUMMARY
AND THE FUTURE

This book is a brief summary of crannog research in Scotland. The important work of the nineteenth century showed how much interest there was in the subject and the range of sites that were examined at that time. The researchers then made a significant contribution to the subject and produced excellent results given the restrictions they worked under. Even with these problems they produced plans, drawings and records of many sites. They recognised the common identifiers that are still looked for by today's surveyors when examining new sites. They explained the excellent state of preservation that the sites offered and they produced many reports that make enlightening and entertaining reading. Overall they created a solid base for later research.

The few excavations carried out in the first half of the twentieth century have been outlined with their varying standards and results. There was a clear development in scientific standards and archaeological understanding from the time of Fraser's excavation at the Loch of Kinellan in 1917, to Piggott's excavations at Milton Loch in 1950. Piggott was one of the first archaeologists to use radiocarbon dating and demonstrated one of the most useful techniques available to researchers on waterlogged sites today.

Improvements in the equipment for working underwater, and particularly the development of the aqualung after the Second World War, meant that it was no longer so difficult to go into the field to carry out underwater survey. The developments of archaeological techniques underwater, from Ruoff's work in the 1960s to the present, has shown that standards achieved underwater are as professional and accurate as those achieved on land sites.

The excavation of Oakbank Crannog has been, and continues to be, immensely exciting. Work at the site provided the first clear evidence of a crannog built initially as a free-standing pile-dwelling that changed its form and developed into a complex mound of remains over 200 years. Each year there is great anticipation of discovering more objects or eco-facts that are the first examples from archaeological sites anywhere which have enabled us to recreate an incredibly detailed portrayal of life. Working in and around the house of our Iron Age ancestors is like going home to a familiar place and the story of their lives is not fiction but fact.

The landscape that the crannog-dwellers exploited is still recognisable around the shores of Loch Tay but they would not believe the dramatic changes that have taken place in the last 2,500 years. The alder trees and the many wild plants they harvested are still there but now have little value to the modern world except as a kind of natural tourist attraction. Oakbank has shown how selective our ancestors were in their choice of cloudberries from the high hills, hazelnuts, cherries, blackberries and raspberries from around the loch shores and in their dynamic trading for exotic species like opium poppy and selected grain like spelt wheat.

The picture of the Loch Tay crannog folk is one of wealth and status. The very fact that they could build a structure like the crannog reveals a great deal about their power and position within their community. They valued fine clothes as seen by the textile found at Oakbank. They cared about their appearance and valued decorative objects like necklaces, pendants and bracelets as seen by the jet bead, the polished stone bead and the sandstone pendant. The jet bead in particular shows again the desire for trade goods from outside the area.

The excavations at Oakbank Crannog show the tremendous potential for the future of underwater archaeology and crannog research in Scotland. The techniques that have been developed to excavate the site in the last 25 years are now commonplace to the underwater archaeologists who work there and on other sites. If, through the use of these techniques, we have been able to create a complex, exciting and comprehensive description of Oakbank and its people based on the excavation of only half of the site, it is exciting to consider the discoveries that will come from not only the unexcavated half but also the other 17 sites in the loch. One of the most telling points of the Oakbank excavation will be the final excavation to loch-bed level and the final plan of the original site: the first crannog on virgin loch bed, before the build-up of the following 200 years of occupation.

The level of survey and excavation of crannogs in Scottish lochs in the last 25 years has thus ably demonstrated that the range of sites is broad and that the well-preserved organic material allows radiocarbon dates and environmental analyses to be carried out with exciting results but with minimum disturbance to the sites. Prehistoric and Medieval crannogs are now being looked at in depth and the STUA and the University of Edinburgh are in the forefront of that work with young students eager to become involved in the new courses and projects on offer.

There is now a greater opportunity than ever before to work towards a classification of these enigmatic sites. An enhanced record will create the necessary framework to assist with the future protection and management of this vast cultural resource. Progress in crannog research in the future, then, will rely on the recognition of crannogs as a class of monument, continued skills-based development, and a greater allocation of resources to enable further survey and excavation.

UNCALIBRATED RADIOCARBON DATES FROM OAKBANK CRANNOG

	Date BP and Lab No.	BC	Adjusted	Description
1	2545±55 (GU-1323)	595±110	705 - 485	Primary oak penetrating sit
2	2410±60 (GU-1325)	460±120	580 - 340	Lochbed, between mounds
3	2360±60 (GU-1463)	410±120	530 - 290	Alder stake above floor
4	2405±60 (GU-1464)	455±120	575 - 335	Alder stake above floor
5	2490±50 (GU-3468)	540±100	640 - 440	Walkway pile
6	2560±50 (GU-3469)	610±100	710 - 510	Deep trench on south side
7	2510±50 (GU-3470)	560±100	660 - 460	Deep trench on south side
8	2490±50 (GU-3471)	540±100	640 - 440	Fence parallel to shore
9	2450±50 (GU-3472)	500±100	600 - 400	Fence parallel to shore

When calibrated, because of anomalies in the calibration curve for dates in the first millenniu
BC, the dates range from about 800BC to about 300 BC.

REFERENCES AND
BIBLIOGRAPHY

Alcock, L. *Arthur's Britain*. London. 1971.

Armit, I. (ed.), *Beyond the Brocks: Changing Perspectives on the Atlantic Scottish Iron Age*, Edinburgh University Press, 1990.

Andersen, S. Tybrind Vig. *Current Archaeology* 93. 315. 1984.

Andrian, B.L. and Dixon, T.N. *An Underwater Survey of Eilean Loch Tollaidh, Gairloch*. Edinburgh. Report for the Gairloch Heritage Museum. 1992.

Andrian, B.L. and Dixon, T.N. *Lochindorb Survey – August, 1993*. Report for the Lochindorb Heritage Project. 1994.

Barber, J.W. and Crone, B.A. Crannogs: a diminishing resource? A survey of the crannogs of south-west Scotland and excavations at Buiston Crannog. *Antiquity* 67. 520-33. 1993.

Bass, G. F. *Archaeology Underwater*. Thames and Hudson. London. 1966.

Blundell, Rev. F.O. Notice of the Examination, by means of a diving dress, of the Artificial Island of Eilean Muireach, Loch Ness. *Proceedings of the Society of Antiquaries of Scotland* XLIII. 159-64. 1909.

Blundell, Rev. F.O. Artificial Islands in the Highland Area. *Proceedings of the Society of Antiquaries of Scotland* XLVII. 26-7. 1913.

Blundell, Rev. F.O. Artificial Islands in the Beauly Firth, etc. *Proceedings of the Society of Antiquaries of Scotland* XLIV. 12-33. 1910.

Blundell, Rev. F.O. Arisaig, and an artificial island there. *Proceedings of the Society of Antiquaries of Scotland* XLV. 353-66. 1911.

Bocquet, A. Lake Bottom Archaeology. *Scientific American* 240.2. 48-56. 1979.

Campbell, F. Note on an artificial island and ancient canoe found near Tobermory, Mull. *Proceedings of the Society of Antiquaries of Scotland* VIII. 465. 1871.

Campbell, M. and Sandeman, M.L.S. Mid-Argyll: a Field Survey. *Proceedings of the Society of Antiquaries of Scotland* XCV. 1-125. 1964.

Clapham, A.J. and Scaife, R.G. A Pollen and Plant Macrofossil Investigation of Oakbank

Crannog, Loch Tay, Scotland, in Murphy, P. and French, C. (eds) *The Exploitation of Wetlands*, BAR British Series 186. Oxford. 1988.

Colt Archaeological Institute. *Surveying in Archaeology Underwater*. Bernard Quaritch Ltd. London. 1969.

Dean, M. *et al* (eds). *Archaeology Underwater: the NAS Guide to Principles and Practice*. NAS and Archetype books. 1992.

Delgado, J. (ed). *Encyclopaedia of Underwater and Maritime Archaeology*. British Museum Press. 1997.

Dixon, T.N. Ben Lawers Project: Loch Tay Shore and Underwater Survey. In *Discovery and Excavation in Scotland*. Council for Scottish Archaeology. 2003.

Dixon, T.N. *The Crannogs of Loch Tay*. STUA. 2000.

Dixon, T.N. The Crannogs of Scotland in Gage, S. and Mullin, P. (eds) *Zeitgeist: An anthology of popular science writing*. (From Edinburgh International Science Festival). 29-38. Science Reviews Ltd. 1997.

Dixon, T.N. *Archaeology in the Fresh Waters of Scotland*, Maitland P.S., Boon P.J., McLusky D.S. Chichester (eds). 1994a.

Dixon T.N. Reconstructing a Bronze Age Scottish Lake-dwelling, in *Les Sites de Reconstitutions Archéologiques*. Proceedings of a conference at Archéosite d'Aubechies, Belguim. Archéosite d'Aubechies-Beloeil, D/1995/7309/1. 1994b.

Dixon, T.N. The History of Crannog Survey and Excavation in Scotland. *International Journal of Nautical Archaeology*. 20.1: 1-8. 1991a.

Dixon, T.N. Oakbank Crannog, In *University of Edinburgh, Department of Archaeology Annual Report*. 37: 27. 1991b.

Dixon, T.N. Scottish Crannogs and Archaeological Excavation Underwater. *Progress in Underwater Science*. 13: 41-55. 1989a.

Dixon, T.N. Crannogs in south-west Scotland, in *University of Edinburgh, Department of Archaeology Annual Report*. 35: 28-9. 1989b.

Dixon, T.N. Eilean Domhnuill, Loch Olabhat: underwater excavations, in *University of Edinburgh Department of Archaeology Annual Report*. 35: 21-2. 1989c.

Dixon, T.N. Loch Bharabhat, the underwater excavations, in *University of Edinburgh, Department of Archaeology Annual Report*. 35: 19-20. 1989d.

Dixon, T.N. Oakbank Crannog. *Current Archaeology* 90. 217-20. 1984a.

Dixon, T.N. The Crannogs of Loch Tay. *Journal of the Perthshire Society of Natural Science*. 15: 25-30. 1984b.

Dixon, T.N. A survey of crannogs in Loch Tay. *Proceedings of the Society of Antiquaries of Scotland* 112. 17-38. 1982.

Dixon, T.N. Excavation of Oakbank Crannog, Loch Tay: Interim Report. *International Journal of Nautical Archaeology and Underwater Exploration* 11.2. 125-32. 1982b.

Dixon, T.N. Preliminary excavation of Oakbank Crannog, Loch Tay: Interim Report. *International Journal of Nautical Archaeology and Underwater Exploration* 10. 15-21. 1981.

Dixon, T.N. and Andrian, B.L. Social Prehistory of Scottish Lochs, in *British Archaeology*, June. Council for British Archaeology. York. 1996.

Dixon, T.N. and Andrian, B.L. Underwater Archaeology, in Scotland. *Scottish Archaeological Review* Vols 9 and 10. Cruithe Press. Glasgow. 1995.

Dixon, T.N. and Andrian, B.L. *Underwater Survey: Loch of Clunie, Perthshire*. Report for Royal Commission on the Ancient and Historical Monuments of Scotland. 1991.

Dixon, T.N. and Andrian, B.L. Loch Tollie Survey, Gairloch, Ross-shire, in Department of Archaeology *Annual Report*. 38. 1992.

Dixon, T N. and Andrian, B.L. *A Survey of Crannogs in Southwest Scotland*. Report for AOC/Historic Scotland. 1989.

Dixon, T.N. and Andrian, B.L. *Preliminary Excavations Underwater at Eilean Domhnuill, Loch Olabhat*. Report for National Museum of Scotland. 1989.

Dixon, T.N. and Harding, D.W. Dun Bharabhat, Cnip: an Iron Age settlement in West Lewis. *Calanais Research Series Number 2*. University of Edinburgh. 2000.

Dixon, T.N. and Harding, D.W. Loch Bharabhat, Cnip, Isle of Lewis, In *University of Edinburgh, Department of Archaeology Annual Report* 34. 19-20. 1988.

Dixon, T.N. and Topping, P.G. Preliminary Survey of Later Prehistoric Artificial Islands on the Isle of Lewis, Outer Hebrides. *International Journal of Nautical Archaeology*, 15.3: 189-94. 1986.

Earwood, C. The wooden artifacts from Loch Glashan Crannog, Mid Argyll. *Proceedings of the Society of Antiquaries of Scotland* 120. 79-94. 1990.

Edwards, N. *The archaeology of early medieval Ireland*. London. 1990

Fairbairn, A., Excavation of a mediaeval site on Donald's Isle, Loch Doon, *Proceedings of the Society of Antiquaries of Scotland,* 71. 323-333. 1937.

Fraser, H. Investigation of the artificial island in Loch Kinellan, Strathpeffer. *Proceedings of the Society of Antiquaries of Scotland,* 51. 48-98. 1917.

Grigor, J. Notice of the remains of two ancient lake dwellings in the Loch of the Clans. *Proceedings of the Society of Antiquaries of Scotland* V, 116-18. 1863.

Grigor, J. Further explorations of the ancient lake dwellings in the Loch of the Clans, on the estate of Kilravoch, Nairnshire. *Proceedings of the Society of Antiquaries of Scotland* 5. 332-35. 1864.

Guido, M.A. Scottish crannog re-dated. *Antiquity* 48. 54-5. 1974.

Hale, A. Carn Dubh, Phopachy, Redcastle and Coulmore intertidal crannogs, in *Discovery and Excavation in Scotland*. 1994.

Hamilton, J.R.C., Excavations at Clickhimmin, Shetland. Ministry of Public Buildings & Works, archaeological report no.6.

Hansen, P.V., Reconstructing a Mediaeval Trebuchet. Military Illustrated – Past and Present, no. 27. 1990.

Harding A.F. Pavlopetri: A Mycenean Town Underwater. *Archaeology* 23. 242-50. 1970.

Harding A.F., Cadogan G., Howell R. Pavlopetri: Underwater Bronze Age Town in Laconia. *Bulletin of the British School at Athens* 64. 1969.

Harding, D.W. and Topping, P.G. Callanish Archaeological Research Centre. *Annual Report 1*. University of Edinburgh. 1986.

Hawthorne J.G. Port of Corinth. *Archaeology* 18. 191f, 1965.

Heckett, E.W. *Loch Tay Textile*. Report on textile analysis and conservation for STUA. 1990.

Hencken, H.O. Ballinderry Crannog 1. *Proceedings of the Royal Irish Academy* 43 C. 103-239. 1937.

Hencken, H.O. Ballinderry Crannog 2. *Proceedings of the Royal Irish Academy* 47 C. 1-76. 1942.

Hencken, H.O. Lagore Crannog. *Proceedings of the Royal Irish Academy* 43 C. 1-248. 1950.

Henderson, J.C. Islets through time: the definition, dating and distribution of Scottish crannogs. *Oxford Journal of Archaeology* 17 (2). 1998.

Higgins, C.G. Possible disappearances of Mycenean Coastal Settlements of the Messerian Peninsula. *AAA* 70. 23-9. 1966.

Jameson M. H. Excavations at Porto Cheli and vicinity. Preliminary report I. Halieis 1962-1968. *Hesperia* 38. 311-42. 1969.

Jameson M.H. The excavation of a drowned Greek Temple. *Scientific American* 231. 111f. 1974.

Johnstone, Paul. *The Sea Craft of Prehistory*. Routledge. 1988.

Joint Nautical Archaeology Policy Committee. *Heritage at Sea: Proposals for the better protection of archaeological sites underwater*. National Maritime Museum. London. 1989.

Keller, F. *The Lake Dwellings of Switzerland*. Zurich. 1866.

Leatham, J. and Hood, S. Submarine Explorations in Crete. *AAA*. 263-80. 1958.

Lyle, A.A. and Smith, I.R. Running Waters and Standing Waters, in Maitland *et al* (eds) *The Fresh Waters of Scotland*. Chichester. 1994.

Lynn, C,J., Some 'early' ring-foots and crannogs. *Journal of Irish Archaeology* I, 47-59. 1983.

MacKinlay, J., Notice of two 'crannoges' or pallisaded islands, in Bute, with plans. *Proceedings of the Society of Antiquaries of Scotland* 3. 43-6. 1860.

Mapleton, R.J. Notice of an Artificial Island in Loch Kielziebar. *Proceedings of the Society of Antiquaries of Scotland* VII. 322-24. 1867.

Martin, C.J.M. Archaeology Underwater, in *Protection of the underwater heritage*. UNESCO. Paris. 1981.

McArdle, C., McArdle, D. and Morrison, I. Scottish lake-dwellings survey: archaeology and geomorphology in loch Awe, Argyllshire, in *International Journal of Nautical Archaeology* 2.2. 381-82. 1973.

McArdle, C.M. and T.D. Loch Awe Crannog Survey. *Discovery and Excavation in Scotland*. 11-12. 1972.

Miller, J.J., Dickson, J.H. and Dixon, T.N. Unusual food plants from Oakbank Crannog, Loch Tay, Scottish Highlands: cloudberry, opium poppy and spelt wheat. *Antiquity* 72. 805-11. 1998.

Miller, J.J. Oakbank Crannog: building a house of plants. In Smith and Banks (eds) *In the Shadow of the Brochs*. Stroud. Tempus. 2002.

Mitchell, A.,Notice of buildings designed for defence on an island in a loch at Hogsetter in Whalsay, Shetland. *Proceedings of the Society of Antiquaries of Scotland,* 15. 303-15. 1881.

Monteith, J. The Crannog at Lochend, Coatbridge. *Transactions of Glasgow Archaeological Society* 9. 26-43. 1937.

Morrison, I. *Landscape with Lake Dwellings*. EUP. Edinburgh. 1985.

Muckelroy, Keith. *Maritime Archaeology*. Cambridge University Press. 1978.

Muckelroy, Keith (ed). *Archaeology Underwater: An Atlas of the World's Submerged Sites*. McGraw-Hill Book Company (UK) Ltd. Maidenhead, Berkshire. 1980.

Munro, R. *Ancient Scottish Lake Dwellings*. Edinburgh. 1882.

Munro, R. *Lake Dwellings of Europe*. London. 1890.

Munro, R. Ayrshire Crannogs 1. *CAandGAA*, 17-88. 1880.

Munro, R. Ayrshire Crannogs 2. *CAandGAA* 3, 1-51. 1882.

Munro, R. Ayrshire Crannogs 3. *CAandGAA* 4, 1-51. 1884.

Munro, R. Notice of an artificial mound or cairn situated 50 yards within the tidal area of the shore of the island of Eriska, Argyllshire. *Proceedings of the Society of Antiquaries of Scotland* 19. 192-202. 1885.

Munro, R. Crannogs recently discovered in Ayrshire. *Proceedings of the Society of Antiquaries of Scotland* 27. 205-21. 1893.

Murray, J. and Pullar, L. *Bathymetrical Survey of the Freshwater Lochs of Scotland*. Edinburgh. 1910.

O'Sullivan, A. *The Archaeology of Lake Settlement in Ireland*. Discovery Programme Monographs 4. The Royal Irish Academy. Dublin. 1998.

Oakley, G. *Scottish Crannogs*. Unpublished MPhil thesis in Dept of Archaeology, University of Newcastle. 1973.

Pearson, Colin. *Conservation of Marine Archaeological Objects*. Butterworth, London. 1987.

Piggott, C.M. Milton Loch Crannog 1. *Proceedings of the Society of Antiquaries of Scotland* 87, 134-52. 1953

Piggott, S. A Scheme for the Scottish Iron Age, in A.L.F Rivet (ed). *The Iron Age in Northern Britain*. Edinburgh University Press. 1966.

Poidebard, A. *Un Grand Port Disparu: Tyr. Recherches aeriennes et sous-marines, 1934-36.* Bibliotheque archeologique et historique. Paris. 1939.

Pryor, F. *Flag Fen: Prehistoric Fenland Centre.* Batsford/English Heritage. London. 1991.

Raftery, J., Lake Dwellings in Ireland. Scientific Service 4 (3), 5.15. 1957.

Redknap, M. and Lane, A. The Early Medieval crannog at Llangorse, Powys: an interim statement on the 1989-1993 seasons. *International Journal of Nautical Archaeology* 23.3: 189-205, 1994.

Renfrew, J.M., *Palaeoethnobotany.* Methuen, London. 1973.

Ritchie J. The Lake-Dwelling or Crannog in Eaderloch, Loch Treig. *Proceedings of the Society of Antiquaries of Scotland* 76. 8-78. 1942.

Ruoff, U. Palafittes and underwater archaeology. In *Underwater Archaeology a nascent discipline.* 123-38. UNESCO. Paris. 1972.

Ruoff, U. Structures Underwater, in K. Muckelroy (ed) *Archaeology Underwater,* 148-55. McGraw-Hill. London. 1980.

Savory, L. Unpublished dissertation in Dept of Archaeology, Univ of Edinburgh. 1971.

Scott, J.G. Loch Glashan. *Discovery and Excavation in Scotland.* 8-9. 1960.

Scranton, R.L. and Ramage, E.S. Investigations at Corinthian Kenchreai. *Hesperia* 36. 124-86. 1967.

Shaw, J. Shallow water excavation at Kenchreai. *AJA* 71. 227ff. 1967.

Singley, Katherine. *The Conservation of Archaeological Artifacts from Freshwater Environments.* Lake Michigan Maritime Museum, South Haven, Michigan. 1988.

Stuart, J. Notices of a group of artificial islands in the Loch of Dowalton, Wigtownshire, and of other artificial islands or 'crannogs' throughout Scotland. *Proceedings of the Society of Antiquaries of Scotland* VI. 114-78. 1866.

Taylor, J. Du Plat, *Marine Archaeology.* Hutchison. London. 1965.

Throckmorton, Peter. *History from the Sea.* Mitchell Beazley. London. 1987.

UNESCO. *Underwater Archaeology: a nascent discipline.* UNESCO. Paris. 1972.

UNESCO. *Protection of the underwater heritage.* UNESCO. Paris. 1981.

Wilde, W.R., Antiquities recently discovered at Dunshanghlin. *Proceedings of the Royal Irish Academy* 1, 420-6. 1840.

Wilkes, W. St John, *Nautical Archaeology: a handbook.* David and Charles. Newton Abbot. 1971.

Williams, B.B., Excavations at Lough Eskragh, Co. Tyrone. *Ulster Jouranl of Archaeology* 41, 37-48. 1978.

Wilson, G. Crannogs and lake dwellings of Wigtownshire. *Proceedings of the Society of Antiquaries of Scotland* 9. 368-78. 1873.

Wilson, G. Lake dwellings of Wigtownshire 2. *Proceedings of the Society of Antiquaries of Scotland* 10. 737-39. 1875.

Wood-Martin, W.G. *The Lake Dwellings of Ireland*. Dublin. 1886.

LIST OF RESEARCHERS

List of researchers who have carried out work at Oakbank Crannog or work related to the remains from the site. The individuals may no longer be at the institutions where they carried out the analysis or research work and, in some cases, the institutions no longer exist or have different names.

In alphabetical order:

Baxter, I. 1993. Formation of database of crannogs in Scotland. MA dissertation. University of Edinburgh.

Calton, Eric Scottish Centre for Pollen Studies, Napier University, Edinburgh. 1988. Report on environmental sample. Report on Macro- and Micro-scopic examination of sample 6.

Christie, W.W. Hannah Research Institute, University of Glasgow. 1988. Residue analysis. Analysis of residue on wooden dish and identification as butter.

Clapham, Alan. 1988. Macro-plant remains. A Pollen and Plant Macrofossil Investigation of Oakbank Crannog, Loch Tay, Scotland, in P. Murphy and C. French (eds) The Exploitation of Wetlands, BAR British Series 186. Oxford. 1988.

Crone, A.B. 1984. Wood report. Oakbank Crannog: Preliminary Report on the Wood, in T.N. Dixon, Scottish Crannogs. Underwater excavation of artificial islands with special reference to Oakbank Crannog, Loch Tay. PhD thesis. University of Edinburgh. 1984.

Crone, A.B. 1988. Dendrochronology, Dendrochronology and the Study of Crannogs. PhD thesis. University of Sheffield.

Eadie, Emma. 1991. Macro-plant remains. Food production at Oakbank Crannog. MA dissertation. University of Edinburgh.

Hansson, A-M. 1988. Macro-plant remains. Vegetations Historisk Studie från Övergången Bronsålder-Järnålder vid Oakbank Crannog, Skottland. Laborativ Arkeologi 3, Stockholms Universitet.

Heckett, E.W. MA, University College, Cork. 1990. Report for STUA. Loch Tay Textile.

Hunter, W.W. University of St Andrews. 1984. Residue analysis report. Amino acid analysis of burnt residue on pottery.

Jones, Andrew University of York, Environmental Archaeology Unit. 1988. Report on environmental samples. Animal coprolite analysis.

Kenworthy, James University of St Andrews. 1984. Report on stone and flint. Chipped Stone from Oakbank Crannog. Appendix G in T.N. Dixon, Scottish Crannogs. Underwater excavation of artificial islands with special reference to Oakbank Crannog, Loch Tay. PhD thesis. University of Edinburgh. 1984.

Miller, J.J. 1997. Macro-plant remains: An Archaeobotanical Investigation of Oakbank Crannog, a Prehistoric Lake Dwelling in Loch Tay, The Scottish Highlands. Ph.D. thesis. University of Glasgow.

National Museum of Antiquities of Scotland, 1981. Report on slag. X.R.F. analysis of slag.

Sands, R.J.S. 1989. Toolmark signature matching. The Study of the marks left by damaged axes – a multi-faceted approach with particular reference to Oakbank Crannog. BSc dissertation. Institute of Archaeology, University College, London.

Sands, R.J.S. 1994. Toolmark signature matching. Archaeological Potential of Toolmarks on Prehistoric Wood, with Special Reference to Oakbank Crannog, Loch Tay, Scotland. PhD thesis. University of Edinburgh. 1984.

Scaife, R. 1988. Pollen analysis, A Pollen and Plant Macrofossil Investigation of Oakbank Crannog, Loch Tay, Scotland, in P. Murphy and C. French (eds) The Exploitation of Wetlands, BAR British Series 186. Oxford. 1988.

Skinner, Theo National Museum of Scotland. 1984. Report on wood identification. Loch Tay Wet Wood Species Identifications. Appendix C in T.N. Dixon, Scottish Crannogs. Underwater excavation of artificial islands with special reference to Oakbank Crannog, Loch Tay. PhD thesis. University of Edinburgh. 1984.

Smith, Catherine Duncan of Jordanstone College of Art, Dundee. 1984. Report on bone and teeth. A Report on the Animal Remains. Appendix D in T.N. Dixon, Scottish Crannogs. Underwater excavation of artificial islands with special reference to Oakbank Crannog, Loch Tay. PhD thesis. University of Edinburgh. 1984.

Stephens, E. University of St Andrews, 1982. Geological analysis report. Petrology and analysis of slag.

Stokes, Judy. 1981. Macro-plant remains. The potential of underwater environmental archaeology: Oakbank Crannog as a case-study. BSc dissertation, Institute of Archaeology, University College, London.

Tomlinson, Philippa University of York, Environmental Archaeology Unit. 1988. Report on environmental samples. Botanical analysis of samples (including faecal pellets) from Dun Bharabhat and Oakbank Crannogs.

University of Bradford. 1992. Report. Conservation of iron knife.

INDEX